Basic Landscape Construction

Created and Designed by the Editorial Staff of Ortho Books

Project Editors
Robert J. Beckstrom
Sally W. Smith

Writer
Douglas Rossi

Illustrators
Tony Davis
Ron Hildebrand

Ortho Books

Publisher
Robert B. Loperena

Editorial Director
Christine Jordan

Manufacturing Director
Ernie S. Tasaki

Managing Editor
Sally W. Smith

Acquisitions Editors
Robert J. Beckstrom
Michael D. Smith

Prepress Supervisor
Linda M. Bouchard

Sales & Marketing Manager
David C. José

Publisher's Assistant
Joni Christiansen

Graphics Coordinator
Sally J. French

Editorial Coordinator
Cass Dempsey

Copyeditor
Toni Murray

Proofreader
David Sweet

Indexer
Frances Bowles

Separations by
Color Tech Corp.

Lithographed in the USA by
Banta Book Group

Thanks to
Phyllis Calech
Deborah Cowder
Mr. and Mrs. Charles Davis
The Elizabeth F. Gamble
  Garden Center
Will Gorman and Bill Shea
Jeff Hecht, Hecht Construction
Shaunee and Patrick Power
David Van Ness

Photographers
Names of photographers are followed by the page numbers on which their work appears. T=top; C=center; B=bottom; R=right; L=left

William C. Aplin: 17
Scott Atkinson: Front cover BR, 4–5, 20T, 72, 75
Laurie A. Black: 3B, 30–31, 66B
Gay Bumgarner: Photo/Nats: 24T, 33CC, 33BR, 34, 45
Karen Bussolini/Positive Images: 78
Dick Christman: 19T
Alan Copeland: Front cover TR
Stephen Cridland: 66T, 74, 89BR
John Edwards: 64
Barbara J. Ferguson: 81
GE Lexan® Thermoclear™: 80
David Goldberg: 3T, 20B, 33CL, 33CR, 33BC, 48R, 50R, 54, 59, 65, 66C, 89T, back cover TR, back cover BL
Saxon Holt: Front cover LC and LB, 40, 50L, 55, 76–77
Susan Lammers: 33TL, 33TC, 48L
Michael Landis: 24B, 86B, 89BL
Douglas Muir: 13, 33TR
John Neubauer: 1, 8, 9T, 9B, 33BL, 38, back cover TL
Geoffrey Nilsen: Front cover TL, 19BL, 19BC, 19BR, 58B
Ortho Photo Library: Front cover TC, 86T
Kenneth Rice: 56-57
Douglas Rossi: 63, back cover BR
David M. Stone: Photo/Nats: 12
Virginia Twinam-Smith: Photo/Nats: 47
Jessie Walker Associates: 58T

Landscape Designers:
Names of landscape designers are followed by the page numbers on which their work appears. T=top; C=center; B=bottom; R=right; L=left

Patricia V. Angell: 33CL, 33BC, 59, back cover TR
Janan Apaydin, Apaydin Ecoscapes: 33CL, 33BC, 59, back cover TR
Bob Clark: 50R, 65, back cover BL
Mary Gordon: Front cover BR
Barbara Guarino, Lilypons Water Gardens: Front cover LB
Harland Hand: 54
Lon Shapiro: 3T

Front Cover
Building outdoor structures for the landscape involves a variety of skills, from bricklaying to carpentry.

Title Page
When you design constructed elements for your landscape, plan them to support and interact well with the plants and other softscaping elements, as this trellis does.

Page 3
Top: Fences, gates, and paths are some of the first structures that a new landscape calls for.

Bottom: A patio is a welcome addition to any yard.

Back Cover
Successful landscape structures, such as the patios (top left and bottom left), fence (top right), and deck (bottom right) shown here, blend with their settings, so they seem a natural development of the site.

Address all inquiries to:
Ortho Books
Box 5006
San Ramon, CA 94583-0906

1 2 3 4 5 6 7 8 9
96 97 98 99 2000 01

ISBN 0-89721-285-1
Library of Congress Catalog Card Number 95-74578

THE SOLARIS GROUP
2527 Camino Ramon, San Ramon, CA 94583-0906

Basic Landscape Construction

YOUR YARD AS LIVING SPACE

This book is brimming with ideas for your yard, but before you grab your tools and plunge into a construction project, you and members of your family should devote some time to thinking about your entire landscape: the front yard, backyard, side yards, and neighborhood. This chapter will get you started. It presents guidelines for landscape design, tips for planning and budgeting the construction work, and a basic primer of materials and techniques for landscape construction.

The rest of the book is devoted to specific structures, starting with a chapter that teaches you how to plan and build fences, walls, gates, walks, paths, steps, and driveways. The third chapter has ideas for creating a private retreat in your backyard and includes deck and patio designs, techniques for creating shade, and suggestions for making a spa or sauna part of your landscape. In the final chapter, the builder meets the gardener: It's about building things to make gardening easier or more enjoyable and includes ideas for sheds, raised beds, planters, compost bins, and ponds.

A well-designed outdoor living area takes into consideration views, sun, shade, access to the house and to the garden, the proposed uses of the area, and how the structures harmonize with the house and the garden.

YOUR ROOM OUTSIDE

What people call home is more than a building. It includes the land around the house. No matter how large or small your yard is, it offers many exciting opportunities for recreation, relaxation, and visual enjoyment.

Developing a Landscape Design

Just as it takes time to furnish the inside of your home, it takes time to landscape the outside. Several years may pass from the time you start building the structures to the moment you stand and admire the finished landscape.

Flowers will need to be planted, trees will have to grow. You may decide to add landscape projects or even change a few you are not satisfied with. Enjoy the process.

The fundamental considerations when designing a landscape are (1) how you and your family want to use the space and (2) the natural features you have to work with.

The kids may want play space, you may want a deck. Someone else may want flower beds or room for a vegetable plot. All these competing uses must be evaluated and integrated as you begin to plan the landscape. Keep in mind practical matters such as budget, along with how your yard is affected by light, weather, noise, land contours, runoff, and existing foliage. These factors will play a part in formulating your plan.

Considering Uses

Here's an easy way to develop a concept of how you want to landscape your yard.

First, from books, magazines, neighborhood walks, and other sources, collect ideas of things you'd like to see in your own yard. Store and organize these ideas in a central file, such as an accordion file or a three-ring binder. Use this as an idea inventory for discussion with your family as you evolve a landscaping concept.

Next, draw a bubble plan to capture preliminary ideas. This type of plan helps you to focus on your whole yard and keeps you from getting hung up on specific details. To make a bubble plan, first obtain a plot plan or draw a freehand sketch of your property. The plan or sketch should show the fixed structures, such as house, driveway, fences, and walks. Include trees and other natural features. Determine where north is and mark it on your sketch. Show the street and any significant features on the adjacent properties. Make sure to note prevailing winds, shaded areas, low spots that

collect water, and areas that get a lot of light. Also note points of access and patterns of movement—doors, gates, and paths, including footpaths across lawns and other areas.

List your family's needs for the yard. Everyone in the family should contribute ideas. Consider future members of the family and the fact that children's needs will change as they grow. To record ideas, affix a piece of tracing paper over your sketch and hang it where everyone in the family can see it, such as on the refrigerator. Have a pencil nearby so family members can add, scratch out, and revise ideas. To organize and visualize ideas, draw circles (the circles are the reason why it's called a bubble plan) that indicate general use, such as play area, flower beds, or entertainment patio.

This plan will be revised many times. To keep the planning process from getting unwieldy, all family members should agree on some ground rules: a deadline; an agreement to honor all suggestions, even if they are not selected; and an understanding that costs could be the final determinant of what can be done.

Evaluating the Site

Include in your bubble plan those needs that are dictated by the site itself. Begin by separating the public and private areas. To consider areas that can be seen from the street (these areas are often called the public garden), walk and ride past your house. Look critically at both the good and bad points—what real estate

---

Typical Family Needs

An effective landscape meets the most important of your family's needs. To be sure you don't overlook possible uses of your space, review this list.

Outdoor Living Areas
Patio or deck
Outdoor eating area
Outdoor cooking area
Private garden
Secluded reading nook
Sunbathing area
View point

Children's Play Areas
Sandbox
Lawn
Playhouse
Treehouse
Swing set, climbing structure
Wading pool
Racetrack for tricycles
Platform

Recreation Areas
Game court: Tennis, basketball, handball, horseshoes, volleyball
Game lawn: Croquet, putting green, bowling
Exercise circuit
Swimming pool
Spa or hot tub

Utility Areas
Garbage-can garage
Dog run or doghouse
Garden equipment storage
Potting shed
Workshop
Firewood storage
RV or boat storage
Compost area
Extra parking

Specialty Gardens
Vegetable garden
Cutting garden
Herb garden
Garden pool
Rock garden

Sample Bubble Diagram

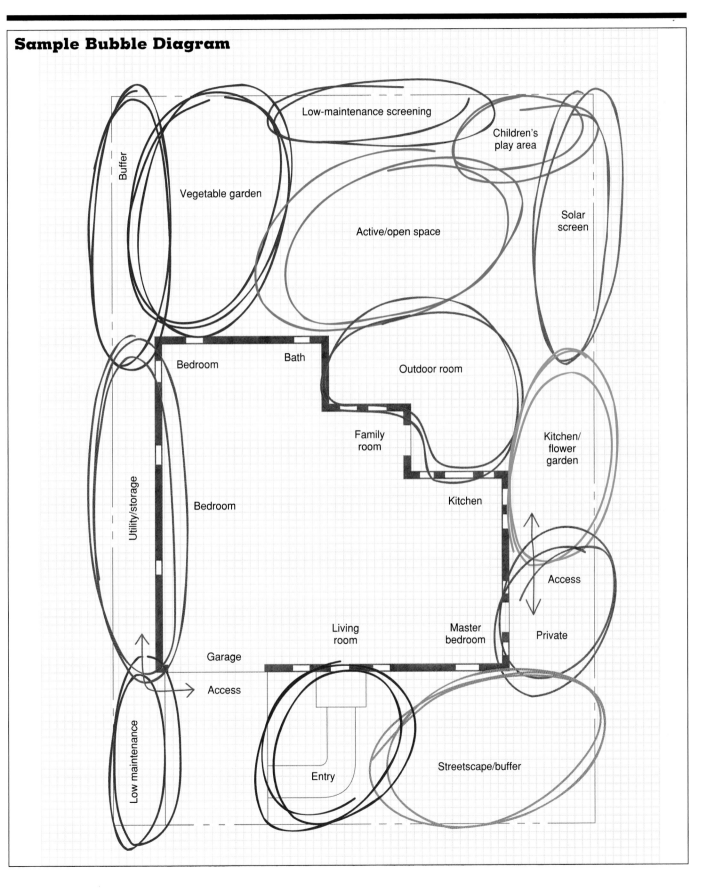

appraisers call curb appeal—and then accommodate them in your bubble plan. For instance, if garbage cans or an air-conditioning unit are visible, plan fences and plant materials to screen them.

Your backyard should be your private retreat. If the neighbor's windows overlook your yard or the yard is exposed to a public sidewalk, think of ways to shield the area from view. The solution could be a fence or tall shrubs.

Buffer areas can be created to reduce noise and wind. Place these along the perimeter of your property. If the area where you're planning to build a deck is exposed to a lot of sun, plan to create shade by planting a tree or erecting an overhead.

Finally, evaluate the existing walks and foot-traffic patterns and how the suggested use areas in your bubble plan may affect them. If your family cuts across the lawn to get to the house, then it may be time to put in a walk to accommodate that traffic.

The Art of Design

Figuring out what you want and developing a bubble plan is easy. Now comes the hard part. Once you've settled on the uses you want to integrate into your plan, then you must concentrate on the design and shape of the actual structures. You don't want to have a hodgepodge of different styles; the trick to landscaping is

having a consistent style. At this stage, consulting with a designer knowledgeable about construction materials and plants can be valuable. Or do research on your own. The rest of this section discusses the issues you need to consider.

Blend With the Environment

One rule of thumb is to integrate your design into the location. Observe what occurs naturally in the area. Adapt to your surroundings. Avoid designs alien to your area. More specifically, choose materials, such as patio paving or fence lumber, that are native to your area or are widely used. If your community has a wide variety of

styles, as many do, you will have more choices. You don't have to imitate, but you should plan structures and landscaping features that blend with the environment.

Consider Perspective

Perspective is the vista from the place the grounds are viewed. The view from a hill gives the viewer a sense of command. In a home landscape, you can create this lord-of-all-you-survey perspective by erecting a deck that overlooks a sloping yard. A level perspective, which draws the eye, makes a viewer feel connected to the scene—for example, when a path from a ground-floor door leads to

This patio and pond blend so successfully with their surroundings that they appear to be natural features of the landscape.

a garden. A different perspective occurs when the grounds are below grade. Standing in a sunken garden may give a sense of security and intimacy—or of confinement.

Determining Focal Point

Another element of perspective is the imaginary line formed when your eye comes to rest on a prominent object, such as a tree or flower bed. This imaginary line is called the axis of the landscape. A variety of techniques is used to create the axis in formal and informal gardens. It may be a straight geometric line of flower beds or a gently curving path that focuses the viewer's attention on a wildflower arrangement. It could also be something beyond your yard, such as a panoramic view, a hill, or a prominent building; if it is, also create—within the landscape—a focal point that is more immediate and on a smaller scale.

Forcing Perspective

Your sense of perspective is influenced by your awareness of what is in the foreground, middle ground, and background. Planting a large tree in the foreground and a smaller one in the background will make your yard seem longer than it is; reversing the two will make the yard seem more compact. This is known as forcing the perspective. Other devices for forcing perspective are variable fence heights, variable sizes of foliage on plants of equal size, and edgings that converge or diverge slightly rather than remain parallel.

Top: This deep yard has been landscaped to create foreground, middle ground, and background elements.
Bottom: Curving flower beds shape a path of lawn that leads the eye to the focal point, a charming gazebo.

PLANNING A PROJECT

Before starting this stage you and your family should have completed "bubble planning," so you have final decisions on how to use the yard space. Now you are going to finalize your plans with a working drawing of your project and a written description of each segment of the work.

Putting Your Plan on Paper

At this stage you may decide that something is missing from your design and opt to employ the trained eye of a landscape architect or landscape designer. This may be less expensive than you expect. First, you will be able to hand the consultant the bubble plan, which shows what you want, so he or she will not have to begin the planning and drawing from scratch. In addition, all you may need is only a consultation and some simple sketches, rather than a formal drawing. If you are going ahead on your own, proceed with the steps that follow.

The Base Plan

Here's where you draw an accurate map, or base plan, of the site. It will take time and seem tedious, but it is an essential step. You'll need graph paper, tracing paper, ⅛-inch scale ruler, pencils, erasers, and a long tape measure (a 100-foot tape is preferred). Using the 100-foot tape, measure the perimeter of your property and the distance from the sides of your house to the property line; then accurately draw your house and property lines on the graph paper. A short cut is to use your property survey, if you have one, to obtain the measurements.

Now measure and add all the other significant features. Include the doors and windows of the house; note the location of exterior faucets and electric outlets; outline the trees, driveways, and paths; and mark the location of any underground utilities. Make sure your plan shows which direction north is.

Working and Detailed Drawings

Once the base plan is completed, draw in the elements that are to be added: decks, patios, walks, raised flower beds, fences, electrical outlets, lighting, trees, shrubs, plants, and so on. Now you have a working drawing.

The next step is to make a detailed drawing of each new component. If you are adding a deck, for example, your drawings will show the footings, piers, posts, beams, joists, and even the railings. Making these detailed drawings will help you visualize each step of the project. No matter how complicated a

Using Your Computer

A good way to draw the base plan and working drawings is to use landscape-drawing computer software. Programs for the various computer formats are available at reasonable cost.

Even using a computer, drawing the base plan will take time. But once you have done that, the computer offers several advantages. You can make changes without redrawing; you can be extremely precise with measurements; it can automatically calculate the size of areas; and you can easily produce copies of plans and drawings to give to the local building department when applying for a permit.

Landscape-drawing programs feature libraries of symbols for trees and shrubs, along with architectural symbols for elements such as outdoor furniture, pools, and patios. Some programs allow you to create side elevations and 3-dimensional views of your plan as well. Other programs can help you design your own deck and other construction projects and help prepare materials lists and cost estimates.

project may appear, once it is broken down into individual tasks, it becomes manageable.

The detailed drawings will help you decide what work you can do yourself and what work you will hire someone else to do. (You will make final decisions about this later in the planning process.) They can also accompany your applications for building permits. In addition, the detailed drawings will help you in the next step: preparing the written description of the work.

Written Description of Work

After completing the detailed drawings, make a list of each construction category (such as excavation, concrete work, masonry, electrical work) in the entire landscape construction job. Then, for each category, list each project in the construction process. Be sure to itemize the structures that will be affected. For example, if several projects require concrete work (deck footings, patio slab, steps, and so on), list all of them under "Concrete work." The following list includes most common construction categories, with applicable projects and structures.

- Site preparation: Removing trees, brush; demolishing structures; building berms
- Excavation: Digging holes, trenches, slab bases
- Concrete work: Pouring footings, slabs
- Masonry: Building walks, patios, walls
- Rough carpentry: Building fences, decks, overheads, raised beds, sheds
- Plumbing: Installing irrigation and hose bibs
- Electrical work: Installing low-voltage lighting, outlets, spa connections

Working Drawing of Site Plan

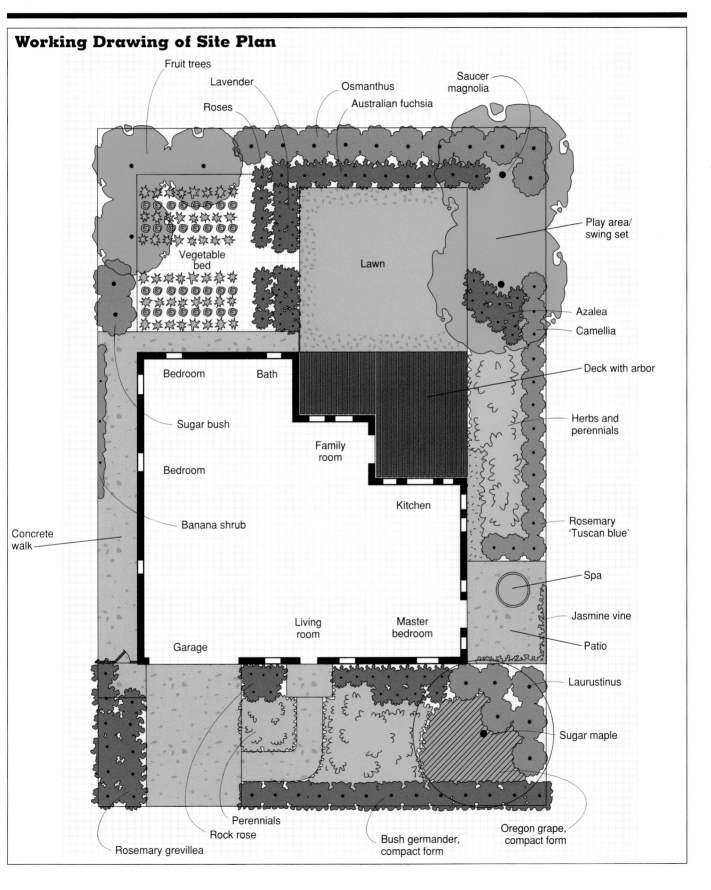

Fruit trees

Lavender

Roses

Osmanthus

Australian fuchsia

Saucer magnolia

Play area/ swing set

Vegetable bed

Lawn

Azalea

Camellia

Deck with arbor

Bedroom

Bath

Sugar bush

Herbs and perennials

Family room

Bedroom

Kitchen

Banana shrub

Rosemary 'Tuscan blue'

Concrete walk

Spa

Jasmine vine

Living room

Master bedroom

Patio

Garage

Laurustinus

Sugar maple

Perennials

Rock rose

Rosemary grevillea

Bush germander, compact form

Oregon grape, compact form

• Finish carpentry: Building railings, trim

• Site finishing: Seeding and planting

This written description of the work to be done will help you see at a glance where you can save time, effort, and money by doing parts of several projects at the same time—even if you don't plan to finish the projects at the same time. You might, for example, decide to pour all the concrete at once. A written description of the work can be especially helpful if the landscaping consists of many projects or will be done in several phases over a long period. If the total job is particularly complex, you may even want to prepare a written description of each project in every category. This will help ensure efficient use of resources.

Who Will Do the Work?

Your first major decision in turning your plan into reality is whether to hire professionals, to do the work yourself, or to do certain parts yourself and hire contractors for the rest. An important consideration is an honest assessment of your own skills and capabilities. Are you handy with tools and knowledgeable about basic construction? Can you do the work quickly and do you have the time? Many homeowners enjoy doing landscape construction projects because they tend not to intrude on the home and they usually aren't as demanding as indoor remodeling. Doing it yourself can certainly save money. In weighing such advantages, be sure to consider the disadvantages, such as taking two months to build a deck while your family is complaining because the yard has been turned into a mess.

Hiring Professionals

Suppose you've decided to hire someone—but who? The best references come by word of mouth from friends and neighbors. Another source is the local garden shop, which probably has a list of recommended landscape architects, designers, and contractors. Another way to find competent help is to drive around and look at how other homes are landscaped. When you find something you like, ask the owner who designed and installed it. Many times people are happy to give a recommendation.

Another decision you need to make involves the kind of landscape professional you need. Each offers different services.

• Landscape architects are similar to building architects. They usually do commercial work, but many will plan and design a landscape for you. They are expensive. Their end products are detailed drawings, plans, and a written description of the work. They will also supervise the construction of the landscape.

• A landscape designer is someone who has less training than a landscape architect but is experienced with the different plants and materials used in landscaping.

• A landscape contractor is the actual builder of the landscape, the person who uses the plans provided by the landscape architect or designer.

Some firms have the phrase "Designers and Builders" in their names because they have professional architects, designers, and builders on staff.

Before selecting any professional or contractor, always ask for and check three references. Ask the owners if they were satisfied with the contractor's work and attitude. Visit job sites under construction and completed projects.

Ask for and check bank references. Make sure the contractor is financially stable and unlikely to go out of business in the middle of the job. If that happens, you may be stuck paying the suppliers so they won't put liens on your property. And don't forget to demand lien releases when the work is completed!

Bidding

If you solicit bids, the drawings and written description of work become even more important. These documents get the ball rolling because they describe what work you want done. If all prospective contractors base their bids on the same set of plans, bids will be easier to compare. Your documents may not be as polished as professionally prepared construction documents, but they will serve as the starting point. How various landscaping professionals work with you to refine your ideas is one way of helping you decide who you're comfortable working with.

When you've decided whom you are going to hire, thank the other bidders for taking the time to bid. At minimum, use a postcard to notify

Deciding to do the work yourself, and the amount of help available to you, can influence the design and building of a project.

them that you have awarded the job to someone else.

Putting It in Writing

If you decide to use a contractor, you need a contract. Contracts are crucial because they clearly detail who will be responsible for performing what work and for how much. The contract doesn't have to be elaborate—most contractors already have their own form—but do insist on its being well written and thorough. Read it carefully and don't hesitate to ask for more detail. If there are problems later on, you will use the contract to resolve the issues.

The list that follows covers the details a thorough contract contains (not all may pertain to your situation).

• Reference to construction documents—the base plan, working drawings, detailed drawings, and the written description of work

• Statement that the contractor will get a certificate of insurance, which guarantees the contractor is covered for all risks

• Stipulation that the contractor is responsible for obtaining permits, performing the work to code, and getting necessary inspections

• Start and completion dates and a detailed schedule

• Specification of the work you are to perform yourself

• List of all the material or fixtures that you will be supplying

• Payment schedule, with dates that correspond to key completion dates

• Stipulation that the contractor will provide lien releases from all subcontractors

and suppliers before final payment is made

• Specific procedure for handling change orders (usually they must be in writing, not merely verbal)

• Method for resolving disputes

Managing the Project

Completing a landscape construction project successfully requires the management skills of budgeting, estimating, and scheduling.

Budgeting

Before you begin, determine how much you want to spend, not how much it's going to cost. Be realistic about what you can afford and how much is appropriate. There are no hard and fast rules about what percentage of your home's value should be spent on landscaping. Of course attractive, practical landscaping will enhance the value of your property. But that doesn't mean that, if you live in a $280,000 house and spend $20,000 on landscaping, you'll get $300,000 if you sell. When figuring how much to spend, always keep in mind what similar homes in your neighborhood are selling for and how much you spent on your house. Remember too that you are considering your home, not just an investment; install the type of landscaping that you will enjoy.

Estimating

After deciding how much you can spend, estimate what all the landscaping improve-

ments will cost. There are several ways to do this, such as finding out the cost of comparable projects or getting competitive bids (get bids only if you truly intend to hire someone). If you do your own estimate, cost out each piece of work by itemizing the materials, rental equipment, and labor required, then getting accurate prices for each item. Use your plan and the written description of work to help you break down each segment into individual cost categories. Make a materials list that includes all lumber and price it out at several lumberyards. Make sure to ask if delivery is included. The same goes for masonry, plumbing, electrical work, and nursery stock. Don't forget "hidden" costs, such as tool purchases; deliveries; debris removal; permit

fees; and repair of lawns, fences, sprinklers, and so on that may be damaged.

Scheduling Work

Use your work description to establish a time line, so you can estimate when certain tasks must be started and should be completed. The key to scheduling is to coordinate all the different stages so that, before you start one, all the phases leading up to it are completed. Another trick is to bunch certain jobs together—for example, footings. If you have three projects that will require concrete footings (fence, deck, and stairs, perhaps), then dig all the holes, have the building inspector check them for proper depth, and have all the concrete poured at the same time.

Even if you do all the work yourself, taking time to plan, budget, and schedule your work will help it go more smoothly.

BASIC CONSTRUCTION TECHNIQUES

In this section you'll learn about the materials and techniques you can use to build your landscaping projects. You'll also find specifics on how to estimate and order your materials, and tips for preserving and maintaining outdoor structures.

Safety

Finishing your project without a trip to the doctor or local emergency room should be just as important a goal as doing quality work. No matter how small the project, observe the safety precautions that would apply to a major job site.

•When using a power saw or other power tool, *always* keep your eyes on the work.

•Wear safety glasses when doing anything that might produce eye injuries.

•Don't do heavy work in sneakers. Wear construction boots that provide ankle support and protection from nails and dropped lumber.

•Wear a dust mask when creating dust.

•Don't wear loose clothing or have loopy shoelaces. Anything that might catch can cause falls—or worse, get wrapped up in machinery.

•Use knee pads when kneeling.

•Don't leave tools or supplies on top of a stepladder, where they are easily forgotten and just above eye level. They could cause a nasty surprise when you move the ladder.

•Know your limitations and recognize fatigue. After a long busy day, don't try to do "one more project." Quit and do it another day.

•Guard against electrocution. All outdoor electrical outlets should be protected with ground fault circuit interrupters (GFCIs). Power tools should be double insulated.

Tools

You don't need to own all the tools you see in the workshops of those popular home-improvement television shows. A few basics are all that are required. Here are some tips about tools.

•Buy the best quality you can afford. Cheap tools, especially cheap power tools, often break or burn out when you are right in the middle of a project.

•Tools tend to disappear on construction sites. Mark your tools with your name and don't leave them lying around when not in use.

•If you are going to be making miter cuts, splurge and buy an electric miter box. What you spend on one will be amply justified by the time you save by not having to struggle with misaligned miters.

•Add a portable workbench and a few C-clamps to your tool kit. Besides being a convenient place to set up work, the clamping capabilities of the bench will act as an invaluable third hand.

Before You Dig

There's always the chance of finding buried treasure when you dig a hole, but you will more likely encounter a major headache if you don't do some preliminary investigating. If you have a septic system, make sure you know the location of the tank or cesspool and the leach lines. You don't want to disturb any of them when you dig, and you don't want to build a structure over them that will interfere with servicing. Look for evidence of other buried pipes or wires: downspouts that terminate below ground or electrical conduit that goes into or emerges from the ground. Call local utility companies to ask about the location of underground electric, gas, phone, or cable lines—especially if you are excavating near your property line. Most companies will send someone out to mark the locations. Finally, always be careful about excavating below the house foundation. Be wary of digging any trench along the foundation that is deeper than the footings, as it could weaken the foundation.

•Working with dull blades is unprofessional and dangerous. Always use sharp blades and drill bits in your power tools. Dull ones cause the tool to work harder, overheat, and reduce its life span. Always clean blades, bits, and tools before putting them away.

•Own a 100-foot heavy-duty power cord.

•Use a tool belt when working. You'll be less likely to misplace your hand tools if you keep them in the belt. For carrying around many small tools, a 5-gallon plastic bucket makes a handy toolbox.

•Visit your local tool rental agencies to see what hand and power tools are available. You may find an electric jackhammer for breaking up an old patio, a power auger for digging fence posts, a ditch digger for installing a drainage system, or a pneumatic nailer for nailing dozens of fence boards quickly. Whenever you rent a tool, ask the dealer for instructions about safe and proper use.

Site Preparation

Removing existing structures, grading, controlling weeds, digging footings, and installing drainage systems are all part of site preparation. Improper site preparation can lead to sagging decks, standing water in your garden, and other headaches.

Grading and Excavating

Grading means purposefully moving dirt on the surface to create the desired elevation. Removing dirt below the grade is called excavating. In large projects, these processes involve sophisticated engineering. In home landscaping, they are rarely major tasks. The most extensive grading you'll probably have to do is

Basic Tools

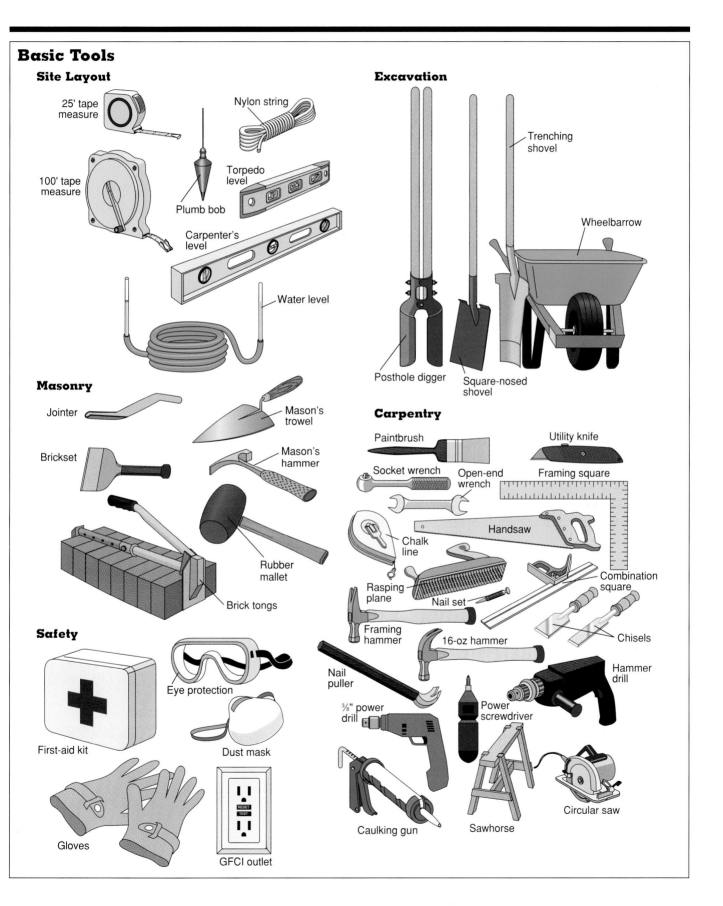

Site Layout

- 25' tape measure
- 100' tape measure
- Nylon string
- Plumb bob
- Torpedo level
- Carpenter's level
- Water level

Masonry

- Jointer
- Brickset
- Mason's trowel
- Mason's hammer
- Rubber mallet
- Brick tongs

Safety

- First-aid kit
- Eye protection
- Dust mask
- Gloves
- GFCI outlet

Excavation

- Trenching shovel
- Wheelbarrow
- Posthole digger
- Square-nosed shovel

Carpentry

- Paintbrush
- Utility knife
- Socket wrench
- Open-end wrench
- Framing square
- Chalk line
- Handsaw
- Rasping plane
- Nail set
- Combination square
- Chisels
- Framing hammer
- 16-oz hammer
- Nail puller
- Hammer drill
- 3/8" power drill
- Power screwdriver
- Caulking gun
- Sawhorse
- Circular saw

15

Some Recommended Footing Depths*

City	Depth
Albany, NY	42"
Albuquerque, NM	18"
Anchorage, AK	42"
Bangor, ME	48"
Camden, NJ	30"
Charleston, WV	24"
Columbus, OH	32"
Fort Worth, TX	6"
Greensboro, NC	12"
Helena, MT	36"
Knoxville, TN	18"
Los Angeles, CA	12"
Minneapolis, MN	42"
Omaha, NB	42"
Seattle, WA	16"
Shreveport, LA	18"
Tampa, FL	6"

*Requirements may vary; check local building code.

leveling ground for a lawn, sloping soil away from the house, or creating a berm. Digging postholes for fences, footing holes for decks, and shallow bases for patios are also typical. Although you can do this work with a shovel, pick, and wheelbarrow, renting a suitable machine is a practical alternative. Backhoes, power augers, trenchers, scoop loaders, and jackhammers are available for rent.

If you are digging footings for deck supports, make sure they are below the frost line, the lowest depth at which the ground freezes. Since you probably had to get a building permit for your deck, make sure you call the building inspector to check and approve the depth of your footing holes *before* concrete is poured. Fail to do this and the inspector will probably make you dig out the concrete.

To estimate the amount of dirt you'll be moving, calculate the number of cubic yards. For a rectangular hole, this involves multiplying the length (in feet) by the width (in feet) by the height (in feet). Then divide the product by 27 (the number of cubic feet in 1 cubic yard). One cubic yard of dirt weighs about 2,200 pounds. For circular holes, use the formula for calculating the volume of a cylinder: $\pi \times r^2 \times$ height.

Drainage

To prevent standing water from collecting in the yard, you may need to construct garden drains. (Drains are especially important if water is collecting close to the home.) These are simply trenches, about 18 inches deep, in which clay or polyvinyl chloride (PVC) plastic

Estimating Dirt to Be Removed

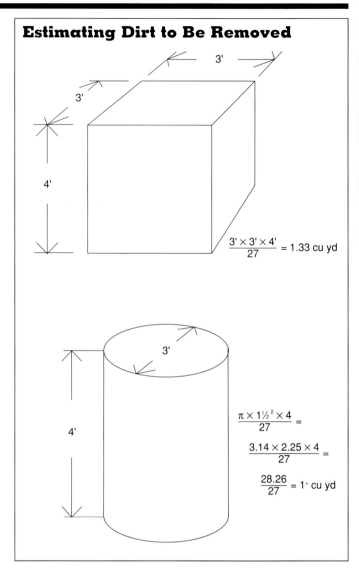

$$\frac{3' \times 3' \times 4'}{27} = 1.33 \text{ cu yd}$$

$$\frac{\pi \times 1\frac{1}{2}^2 \times 4}{27} =$$

$$\frac{3.14 \times 2.25 \times 4}{27} =$$

$$\frac{28.26}{27} = 1^+ \text{ cu yd}$$

Building a Dry Well

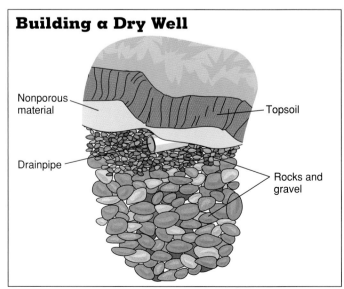

Nonporous material

Topsoil

Drainpipe

Rocks and gravel

drainpipe is laid in a bed of drain rock. To prevent dirt from clogging the pipes, lay old mineral roofing or plastic sheeting over the upper layer of drain rock. Connect the drainpipe to unperforated pipe. Slope both portions toward the collection point, which can be a natural drainage channel or a below-ground dry well. A dry well, or soakaway, is a hole, about 4 feet deep by 3 feet across, filled with large stones, brick, and other hard rubble. It is covered with about 4 inches of gravel, a membrane to prevent soil from filtering into the rocks, and 6 inches of topsoil.

Working With Wood

Choosing the right kind of wood, and fastening it properly, are important factors in determining how your projects will look and how long they will last. Many species, grades, and finishes of wood are available. For outdoor construction the most important distinction is between wood that will come in contact with the ground and wood that will not touch the ground. For ground contact, use only pressure-treated wood specified for ground contact or all-heart grades of a durable species, such as redwood, cedar, or cypress. For above-ground applications, you have a broader choice, although nondurable species of wood must be protected with paint, preservatives, or sealers.

Fasteners—nails, screws, and hardware—used for outdoor projects must be corro-

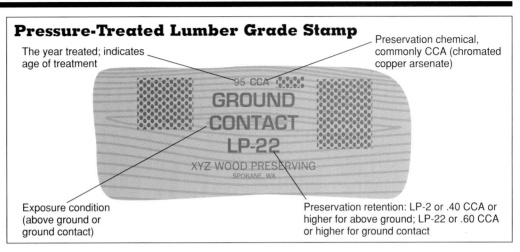

Pressure-Treated Lumber Grade Stamp

The year treated; indicates age of treatment

Preservation chemical, commonly CCA (chromated copper arsenate)

95 CCA

GROUND CONTACT LP-22

XYZ WOOD PRESERVING
SPOKANE, WA

Exposure condition (above ground or ground contact)

Preservation retention: LP-2 or .40 CCA or higher for above ground; LP-22 or .60 CCA or higher for ground contact

sion resistant. They should be zinc-coated (galvanized) or made from stainless steel or aluminum.

Types and Grades of Lumber

Hardwoods—such as oak, cherry, and teak—are most often used for furniture, cabinetry, floors, and other interior applications.

Softwoods—such as pine, hemlock, and fir—are used for framing, millwork, and paneling. Some softwoods (redwood, cedar, and cypress) are naturally rot resistant and are used for siding, exterior trim, decks, fences, and other outdoor structures. Softwoods that are not naturally rot resistant, such as pine and Douglas fir, can be treated with preservatives applied under pressure. Such wood, used widely for outdoor construction projects, is specified for either ground contact or above-ground use.

Pressure-treated Wood

Chromated copper arsenate (CCA) preservative is used to protect wood from termite attack and decay. Above

In lumberyards, lumber is stacked and sorted by species, grade, size, and length.

ground, use wood treated to .25 of CCA per cubic foot (pcf). Posts that touch the ground should be treated to .40 per cubic foot. Most pressure-treated wood is suitable for any outdoor use, such as fences, decks, planters, benches, and play structures. Follow the manufacturer's instructions for the proper use and handling of pressure-treated lumber. A consumer information sheet should be available where the lumber is sold.

Grades

The strength and appearance of lumber are graded according to criteria established by several independent agencies. The two major quality categories are select and common. Select lumber is used when appearance and finishing are important and includes the grades A through D.

• A select grade: Contains no knots

• B select grade: Is devoid of any but minute blemishes

• C select grade: Has some minor defects, such as small knots or blemishes

• D select grade: Has larger blemishes that can be concealed with paint

Common lumber, which is used for framing and structural work, is divided into four categories: select structural, structural joists and planks, light framing, and stud. The grades of common lumber range from 1 to 5, with 1 being the best. Grade 1 common lumber has tight knots and few blemishes.

For most purposes you need know only about light framing lumber, which is the most widely used. Light framing lumber is sold in three categories.

• Construction grade: Top-of-the-line lumber

• Standard grade: Almost as good as and cheaper than construction grade

• Utility grade: Low-quality wood unsuitable for framing

Building codes usually require lumber used in construction to be standard grade or better.

Wood Seasoning

When cut, wood is green and has a high moisture content. Green wood will warp and shrink as it dries, causing problems for structures made with it. To reduce moisture content before it is sold, wood is either air-dried (cutting moisture to 14 to 18 percent) or kiln-dried (which lowers moisture content to 6 to 9 percent). Air-dried lumber is suitable for framing. Kiln-dried wood is preferred where appearance is important, such as in intricate trim or railings. Avoid lumber stamped "S-GRN," except for rustic structures. Look for lumber stamped either "S-DRY" or "MC-15" (moisture content 15 percent).

Plywood

Plywood is sold in 4×8 foot sheets and comes in several thicknesses. The most common are ⅜ inch, ½ inch, ⅝ inch, and ¾ inch. Plywood is graded for interior or exterior use.

Plywood grades are established by the American Plywood Association. For outdoor projects use exterior-grade plywood because the glue used to bond the wood veneers is waterproof. The large capital letters stamped on the sheet tell the grade of its face and back. The grades of plywood follow.

• N: The surface has a natural finish, free of defects.

• A: The wood is smooth and paintable.

• B: A B-grade surface contains small knots.

• C: The surface contains several knotholes and splits of limited size.

• D: A D-grade sheet contains the flaws of a C-grade sheet, but the flaws are larger.

After the stamped grade letter is the group number, which shows the species group used and the relative strength ranging from Group 1 (the strongest) to Group 5.

When cutting plywood with a portable power saw, always have the better side facing down. If you want to avoid splintering either face, apply masking tape along both sides of the proposed cut. While sawing, use a nail or wood chip to keep the cut from closing after the saw blade and pinching it.

Estimating and Ordering Lumber

If you are planning a fairly simple project, such as a shed or playhouse, the best way to estimate your lumber needs is simply to measure and count all the pieces of the same size that the plans call for. On architectural drawings for larger projects, a lumber list should be included. If you have a problem estimating your lumber needs, ask a salesperson at the lumberyard to work out a list for you.

The conventional way of listing lumber is to indicate quantity, then dimension, then length, then species and grade. For example, "seven 2×6×10 PT pine" means seven 2×6s, 10 feet long, of pressure-treated pine. However, lumberyards usually group lumber by species and grade, then dimension, and finally length, so it is easier to ask for "Pressure-treated pine, 2×6, 10 feet long, seven pieces."

Minimizing waste is key to keeping costs down. If your plans show that you need two 5-foot 2×4s, buy one 10-foot 2×4 and cut it in half rather than buying two 6-footers.

When you need to buy a large amount of lumber, such as the lumber for a deck, call several yards and give them your complete lumber list. You may be surprised at the variations in cost.

Fastening the Lumber

Nails, bolts, screws, and hangers are the common devices for fastening lumber together. Knowing which kind to use will make a big difference in how long your project will hold together. Here are some guidelines for choosing and using fasteners.

• Use only hot-dipped galvanized, aluminum, or stainless-steel nails and screws for outdoor projects. Other types will rust and stain the wood.

• Screws and nails should be three times as long as the thickness of the board or part being fastened.

• Common and box nails have more holding power than finishing nails.

• Don't drive finishing nails all the way; otherwise, the wood will be dimpled. Stop driving the nail when it is almost flush and then finish it with a nail set (a heavy common nail can serve as a set).

• Avoid driving nails along a straight line with the grain of the wood. Stagger them and the wood will be less likely to split.

• Before using wood screws, it may be necessary to first make a small pilot hole with a drill. If the screw is difficult to turn with a screwdriver, soap the threads.

Masonry

Few building materials are as simple and basic—and at the same time as elegant, versatile, and durable—as brick and stone. These materials are enduring and give a satisfying appearance of permanence. Selecting the brick or stone for your landscaping is a subjective decision that begins with educating yourself about the local availability of materials and the techniques of this ancient trade.

First visit several masonry supply yards. You'll be surprised at the different kinds of brick, stone, and tile and you'll probably see examples of several kinds of patterns for each. Your decision about which materials to use will be influenced by two factors: your budget and what you think will be attractive. Walk around each yard and look at what is available. When you find something you like, ask the manager what the basic delivery unit is and how much coverage you can expect. At one yard, for

Before ordering concrete blocks, visit the masonry yard to find out what colors, sizes, cell configurations, and specialty blocks—such as end blocks—are available.

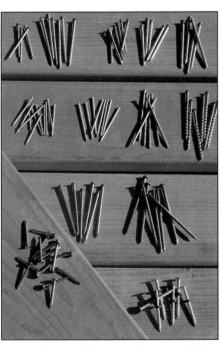

Types of fasteners, from top to bottom, and left to right in each photograph:
Left: Nails commonly used for deck construction are galvanized box, galvanized common; galvanized finish, spiral; stainless steel common, ring shank; joist hanger, grommeted spiral.
Center: Bolts and screws useful in deck construction include carriage bolts, with nuts and washers; machine bolts, with nuts and washers; deck screws, malleable washers, lag screws, and washers.
Right: Framing connectors found in most decks are post cap, post anchors; post caps; hurricane straps; joist hangers, angles; L-brackets, stair angles.

Red and green are complementary colors, which makes brick a natural choice for projects around the garden. Its modular pattern also works well with other repetitive patterns and textures. Bricks can be installed with mortar joints, over a concrete slab (top), installed over a sand base with sand or soil between the bricks (bottom), or butted tightly together over a sand base.

example, Pennsylvania flat rock (used for building low walls) is sold in 1½-ton pallets, from which you could build a 24-foot-long wall 1 foot high; one pallet costs $165. Be sure to ask if the supplier charges for delivery.

Brick

In landscape construction, brick is used for building walls, walks, patios, steps, planters, and grills. A different kind of brick is used for each application.

• Building brick, or common brick, is the kind used for garden construction.

• Paving bricks are slightly larger than building bricks and are much harder. They're used for paving and are recommended for brick-on-sand projects, such as patios and driveways.

• Firebrick, yellow in color, is made to withstand high heat and is used to line grills and fireplaces.

• Face brick is used where a finished appearance is needed. At least one side is smooth, textured, or even glazed.

Another kind of brick is reclaimed, or used, brick. Reclaimed bricks are taken from a demolished building. Usually they can be bought from a demolition contractor or a brickyard. Advantages to their use are that they are cheaper than new brick and are already weathered. When working with reclaimed bricks, be sure to examine each one for cracks and defects.

Building, or common, brick is divided into three grades according to hardness and ability to withstand weathering.

Standard Brick Dimensions

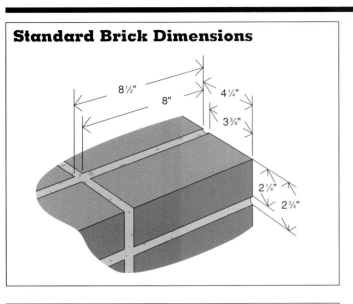

Estimating Bricks and Mortar for a Brick Wall

Materials Required Per 100 Sq Ft Surface Area				
			Mortar Ingredients (mixed 1:3 by volume)	
Thickness of Wall	Number of Bricks	Amount of Mortar	Masonry Cement	Sand
4 in.	616	9 cu ft	3 sacks	9 cu ft
6 in.	1,232	21 cu ft	7 sacks	21 cu ft

• SW, the grade assigned to brick that can withstand severe weathering, is the grade used for contact with the ground or in any areas where frost occurs.

• MW, the grade of brick for moderate weathering, can be used for ground contact in moderate climates.

• NW, the grade of brick that withstands no weathering, should be used indoors or in fully protected areas.

Estimating

Bricks come in several sizes, so it is important to know what the local brickyard stocks. Building bricks are usually 2¼ inches high, 3¾ inches wide, and 8 inches long. These actual dimensions are smaller than the nominal size of a brick (2½ inches by 4 inches by 8½ inches), which takes into account a ¼-inch layer of mortar on each side.

To estimate the number of bricks needed, first figure the surface area of the project in square feet (length × height). Allow 6 bricks per square foot. For walls whose widths consist of two layers, or wythes, double the estimate. Don't forget to allow for breakage and waste. If in doubt, take your measurements to the brick-

yard and have the salesperson do the estimating.

To figure how many bricks will be used in each course, or row of bricks, divide the length (in inches) by the nominal brick length (8½ inches). When planning a brick project, try to keep the overall dimensions evenly divisible by 8½ or 4¼ inches. By doing this you eliminate unnecessary brick cutting and give the job a neater appearance.

Working With Mortar

Mortar consists of a binder (cement) and clean sand in a ratio of 1 part binder to 3 parts sand. Use only clean water for mixing. Never use salt water or beach sand. For small jobs, buy 60- or 80-pound sacks of dry-mixed mortar.

Mix mortar and sand thoroughly. Add water, a little at a time, and mix until mortar has a uniform color and a smooth texture.

Cutting and Laying Brick

If you are doing work where you need clean cuts, then use a circular saw with a masonry blade. The other, faster, method is to cut the brick with a chisel. Without practice, this is often imprecise and leads to a lot of waste. Be sure to set

Brick Patterns for Paths and Patios

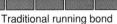
Traditional running bond

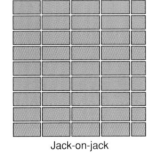
Jack-on-jack

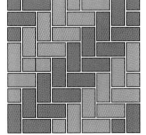
Herringbone

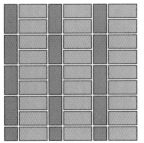
Ladder weave

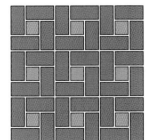
Pinwheel

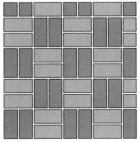
Basket weave

Cutting a Brick

Cutting With a Brickset and Hammer

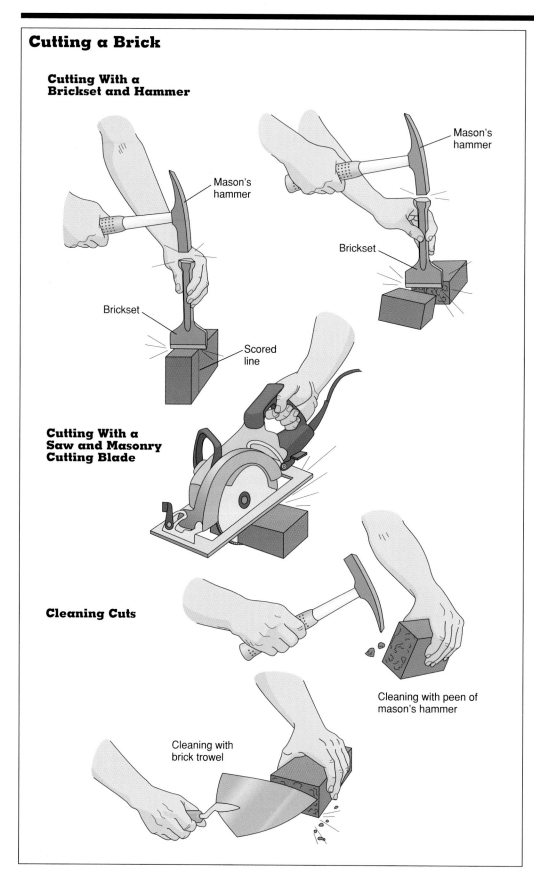

Mason's hammer

Mason's hammer

Brickset

Brickset

Scored line

Cutting With a Saw and Masonry Cutting Blade

Cleaning Cuts

Cleaning with peen of mason's hammer

Cleaning with brick trowel

the brick on a sand bed before striking it.

For a walk or patio, the easiest method of laying bricks is to set them in a bed of compacted gravel and sand (see page 69). A more permanent installation consists of bricks laid over a concrete slab (for walks, see page 52; for patios, see page 68). For building a brick wall, see pages 43 to 45.

Stone

Stonemasonry requires great patience and a certain artistic flair for finding and fitting just the right stone. Working with stone involves finding the right type of stones, cutting them to the needed size, and laying the stone to form a patio or wall.

Stones are sold by the ton and delivered in pallets. Let the supplier calculate how much you need, based on your square-footage measurements.

The six kinds of stone that do-it-yourselfers usually use are bluestone, granite, slate, limestone, sandstone, and marble. In addition, do-it-yourselfers often use manufactured, or artificial, stone. Types of manufactured stone include cast, precast, cultured, imitation, and reconstructed.

Stones fall into three broad categories.

•Flagstone: Irregular shapes and precut squares with a uniform thickness. Popular for walks and patios.

•Fieldstone, or rubble: Irregular shapes (usually round) and thicknesses, used for walls.

•Ashlar: Stone cut on all sides, and uniform in at least one dimension—usually height; used for stacking.

Marking and Cutting a Flagstone

Next stone
to be set

Stones
already set

Stone
to be cut

Cutting line

Groove scored
with brickset or
chisel

Chisel

Pipe or 2×4

Some stones—such as flag-stone, slate, and marble—can be used as veneers over walls built with concrete block.

Building With Stone

The basic tools for cutting stone are a pitching chisel, a 2½- to 3-pound club hammer (or 5-pound sledgehammer), and protective eyewear.

Place the rock on a bed of sand (placing it on concrete will cause it to break, from shock, in the wrong place). Turn the rock and look for existing cracks or defined grain on which to make the split. Score the line to be cut by making a series of small cuts with the chisel. Place a pipe or 2×4 under the line and the chisel on the line; give the chisel one or two sharp raps. Use the hammer and chisel to trim off any uneven surface.

Flagstone is irregularly shaped; some pieces may have to be trimmed when making a walk. Let the next stone to be laid overlap the stone to be cut. Mark the cutting line with a pencil, using the edge of the top stone as the guide (see the illustration at left). Score a ⅛-inch-deep groove along the

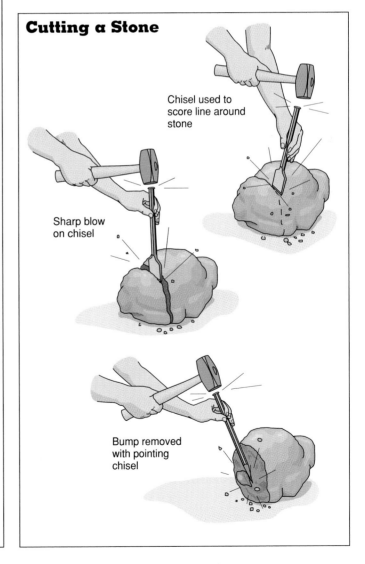

Cutting a Stone

Chisel used to
score line around
stone

Sharp blow
on chisel

Bump removed
with pointing
chisel

pencil line. Place a length of pipe or wood under the stone so the scored line slightly overhangs it. Using the chisel and hammer, strike sharply along the groove. (If the stone is large, you can tap the unsupported part directly, with the hammer.)

Stone walls built with mortar are called mortared, or wet, walls. Those built without mortar are called dry, or loose-laid, walls (see pages 40 to 42). Stone patios and walks should be laid over a concrete base (for patios, see page 68; for walks, see page 52). An informal stone path can be made simply by installing flagstones as stepping-stones. For this type of path, remove the sod and enough soil so the flagstone will sit flush with the surface. Bed the stone in sand to keep it from rocking.

Concrete

Concrete is made from different proportions of portland cement (the "glue"), sand, and gravel. The sand and gravel are called the aggregate. Working with concrete isn't difficult, as long as the projects you are undertaking are manageable. For most do-it-yourselfers, these include pouring piers and footings for decks and creating slab foundations for patios and sheds. Such projects are relatively small and don't need a professional-looking finish. For these jobs, have the right concrete mixture and make sure the excavations are deep enough to be below the frost line. (Get the building inspector's OK before filling the holes with concrete!)

Top: Durable, natural, and versatile, stone is a favorite material for landscape construction because it can achieve so many effects. Here, a rustic stone wall and matching flagstone patio evoke a natural grotto.
Bottom: A small concrete project, such as forming and pouring footings for a deck, is within the capabilities of almost any homeowner.

Crew at a Large Concrete Pour

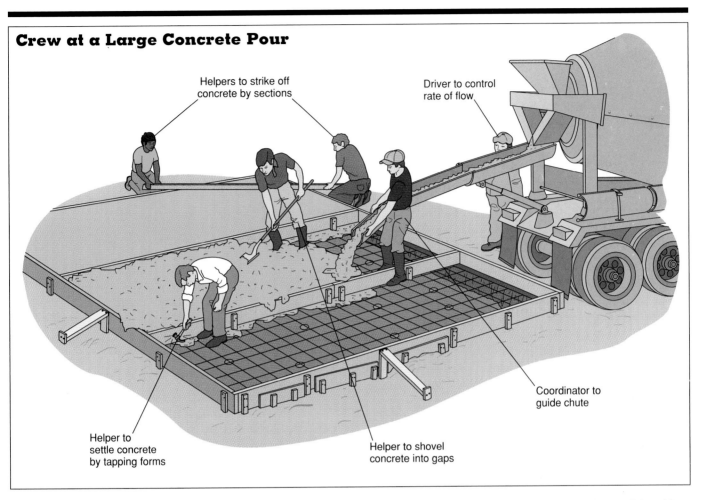

Helpers to strike off concrete by sections

Driver to control rate of flow

Coordinator to guide chute

Helper to settle concrete by tapping forms

Helper to shovel concrete into gaps

Ready for a Big Job?

Large projects—such as a large patio, driveway, or long walk—require some experience, along with a few capable helpers and some specialized tools. Before undertaking a large project, watch a concrete crew in action. A large job requires muscle for excavation and laying a gravel base, knowledge of building forms, and the speed and strength to spread the concrete as it is being delivered. Ask yourself if you can duplicate the work, and if the savings of doing it yourself are worth the effort. Don't forget to add in the cost of tools, rubber boots, and gloves (concrete is caustic).

As important as well-organized pouring is the final stage, finishing. You'll have to look at the finish every day for years to come. No one likes to be reminded of a botched or amateurish job. If concrete isn't finished and cured correctly, you may have an uneven finish, or worse, cracks.

You can tackle a large job if you take time to study and learn the proper technique and have the physical stamina, helpers, tools, and forms to do the work. One way to cut costs on a large job is to do all the site preparation, make the forms, and even schedule the truck, but hire a concrete crew for pouring and finishing.

Basic Concrete Techniques

All concrete work involves at least some of the steps outlined below.

1. Lay out the site with strings and batter boards. Dig the footing holes or slab excavation to the depth required by your local building code. Call the building inspector to approve the holes before the concrete is poured.

2. Build forms, if needed. Usually you don't need forms for deck piers or wall footings; the hole itself will hold the concrete. For a simple patio, use 2×4s for the forms—the slab should be 4 inches thick—set around the edge of the excavation. Structural slabs

(which support walls) and patios where winters are cold require deeper footings around the perimeter, so you will have to build taller forms. After the forms are in place, place 4 to 6 inches of sand or gravel in the excavation and tamp it down so it is level with the bottom of the 2×4 forms. Lay wire reinforcing mesh (referred to as 6-6-10-10 wire mesh) over the base, if needed. Support it on 2-inch dobies so it will be embedded in the center of the slab, not the bottom. Don't forget to lay any electrical conduit or drains. Wet the forms and gravel just before the pour.

3. Estimate how much concrete is needed. For small

Mixing and Curing Concrete

The strength and durability of concrete are determined by the proportion of dry ingredients to water. You can purchase a prepared concrete mix (called a premix), combine the dry ingredients yourself, or order a delivery of ready-mixed concrete.

Using a Concrete Mix

A premix contains all the dry ingredients—cement, sand, and gravel—in the proper ratio. Using concrete mix is fine for small jobs or if you prefer not to take the time to figure, purchase, and combine the dry ingredients. It's easy to mix; all you do is add the right amount of water. The only drawback is that the convenience of the mix increases cost.

One 80-pound bag of concrete mix usually yields approximately ⅔ cubic foot (check bag label). To make 1 cubic yard, you would need to buy 40 sacks. You can mix one sack at a time in a garden wheelbarrow, two sacks in a contractor's wheelbarrow.

Combining Dry Ingredients

For relatively large jobs and to save money, you can mix the dry ingredients yourself. Mix 1 part portland cement, 2 parts sand, and 3 parts gravel (1-inch diameter maximum) with enough water for proper consistency. You can have the dry ingredients delivered or haul them yourself. The chart opposite gives you an idea of the amount of cement, sand, gravel, and water you'll need to make various quantities of concrete.

Mixing Concrete

Mix concrete in a wheelbarrow, metal tub, homemade trough, or rented motorized mixer. Be sure to mix enough concrete in one batch to complete a full section of a pour. If you don't, the first pour will begin to set up and, when the fresh batch is poured on top, "cold joints" will form. These cause overall weakness and cracking.

A shovel makes an excellent measuring scoop for combining dry ingredients or measuring a mix. Be careful when mixing. Try not to splash out any water—this will alter the concrete's consistency. Follow these techniques for hand-mixing.

1. Place the dry ingredients, in the proper ratios, in the mixing container. Mix thoroughly by digging down and pulling the bottom over the top. Pull from one end several times, then from the other end. This also applies to concrete mix, since ingredients may have settled in the bag.

2. Form a depression in the middle of the dry mixture. Pour in part of the measured amount of water. Pull the dry mixture into the water until it is absorbed.

3. Add water a little at a time and continue to mix. Don't add all the water at once; it makes mixing too difficult. With the shovel or hoe, make a series of hacks that leave ridges. Add more water if the ridges look dry and crumbly, more dry ingredients in the proper ratio if they look runny. Always add water or dry ingredients in very small increments.

Curing Concrete

To cure the concrete properly, leave the forms in place for 5 to 7 days. If you're pouring concrete during cold weather, protect it from freezing by covering it with insulation. Once the concrete is completely cured, continue with the job.

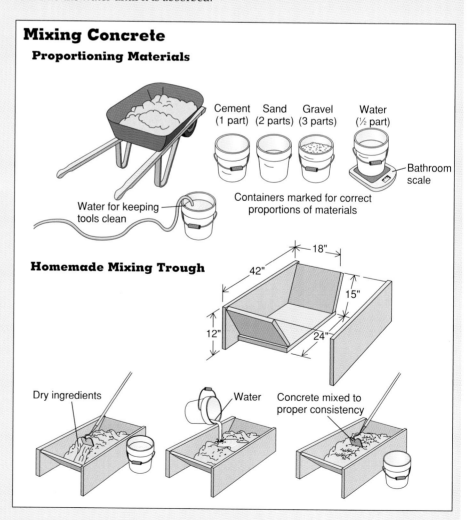

Mixing Concrete

Proportioning Materials

Cement (1 part) Sand (2 parts) Gravel (3 parts) Water (½ part)

Bathroom scale

Water for keeping tools clean

Containers marked for correct proportions of materials

Homemade Mixing Trough

18" 42" 15" 12" 24"

Dry ingredients

Water Concrete mixed to proper consistency

jobs—less than ½ cubic yard—you can combine the cement and aggregate with water and mix it yourself, in a wheelbarrow. If the job needs more than a cubic yard, plan to have a ready-mix truck deliver it. Ready-mix is sold in ¼-yard increments, although there will be a minimum charge for short loads. For ½ to 1 cubic yard, you can mix it yourself or order ready-mix, depending on your experience.

4. If ordering a ready-mix delivery, tell the supplier how much cement you want in the mix, specified as the number of sacks per yard of concrete. Five-sack mixes are used for patios and sidewalks, six-sack mixes for driveways and garage floors. If the truck can't get close enough to the job, arrange to have a pump truck or use wheelbarrows. If you opt for wheelbarrows, have at least two and run wide planks to the site so the wheelbarrows won't sink into the dirt. Wheelbarrow handlers must be strong and fast. Time is money for ready-mix trucks, so if you're not ready to hustle the material and pour, spread, and smooth it, you might as well hire a crew to do the job. On the day of delivery, call the supplier to confirm delivery time.

5. Once the concrete is poured into the forms, it must be consolidated. This is done by jabbing a rod up and down in the mix. Then spread the concrete evenly to the lip of the form—a garden rake will work fine for this.

6. Level the surface with a screed—a 2X4 drawn over the top of the form in a sawing motion. Then float, or smooth, it with a darby or bull float.

7. When the surface is free of water, run an edger between the slab and the form. This is also the time to use either a steel trowel on the surface, for a slick finish, or a wood float, for a nonskid finish.

Concrete needs time to cure, so keep it damp during the first week after the pour. Wet the surface to keep it moist or use plastic sheets to slow evaporation.

Proportions of Ingredients for Making Concrete

	Cu Ft of Concrete				
	4	6	12	18	27*
Cement (90-lb sacks)	1	1½	3	4½	6
Sand (lbs)	200	300	600	900	1,400
Gravel (lbs)	300	450	900	1,350	2,025
Water (gal)	5	7½	15	22½	33¾
or water (lbs)	40	60	120	180	270

* 1 cu yd

Installing Outdoor Receptacles

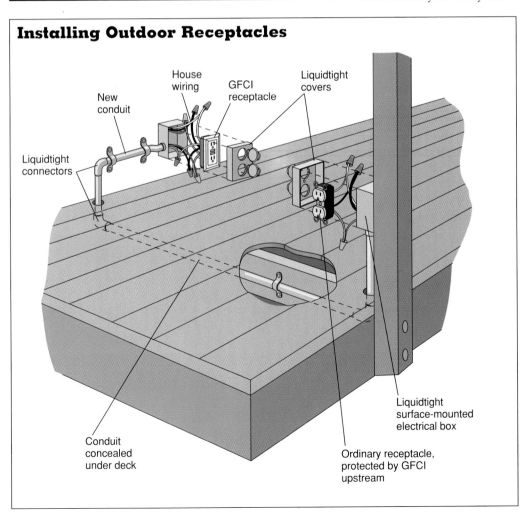

House wiring

New conduit

GFCI receptacle

Liquidtight covers

Liquidtight connectors

Liquidtight connectors

Conduit concealed under deck

Ordinary receptacle, protected by GFCI upstream

Liquidtight surface-mounted electrical box

Outdoor Wiring

Plans for landscape construction are not complete unless they include specifications about electricity. At minimum, the plans should show the electrical outlets you want to add and how you will provide lighting for safety and security. The time to do the basic wiring is in the early stage of construction, when everything is accessible. Of course you can always increase the number of electrical features after the project is complete, but installation may not be as convenient—and the final result may not be as satisfactory—if the features are not part of the original plan.

Wiring Basics

The biggest difference between outdoor wiring and indoor wiring is that outdoor outlets and wiring must be weathertight (referred to as "liquidtight"). If you do any electrical work, it is very important that you be familiar with local and national codes. When finished, but before any work is covered, have it inspected and approved by the building department. The list that follows contains basic information about outdoor wiring. Consult a wiring book or a competent professional for specific wiring techniques.

•Electrical cable run above ground must be encased in metal conduit with liquidtight connectors.

•The two ways to run wiring underground are to (1) fish tape TW or THW wires through metal conduit buried at least 6 inches or through PVC conduit buried at least 18 inches (use metal conduit where it emerges from the ground) or (2) bury Type UF (underground feeder) cable directly in the soil, as long as it's 12 inches deep and covered with boards before the trench is filled (run the cable in metal conduit where it emerges from the ground).

•Metal conduit must be used to protect the cable when it leaves the house and enters the ground.

•Electrical boxes must be liquidtight. Check local code to see which type is permitted.

•All outdoor outlets and fixtures should be on a circuit separate from the main house circuits.

•All outdoor circuits must be protected by a ground fault circuit interrupter (GFCI). The purpose of the GFCI is to kill a circuit the moment there is the potential for electrical shock. If someone happens to touch an appliance, switch, or other fixture on the defective circuit, the GFCI will already have turned the circuit off.

•For lights, use a 15-amp circuit and 14-gauge non-metallic cable. (This kind of cable is marked "14-2, w/G," for 14 gauge, two wires, with a ground.) If you're running a circuit for outlets, use no less than a 20-amp circuit and No. 12 wire. You may need heavier wire, depending on the load and distance.

•Do not attempt to wire swimming pool, spa, or hot tub equipment yourself. These installations must conform to strict electrical requirements and should be wired by a competent professional.

•If you want to avoid having to turn lights on and off with a switch, control them with an automatic timer, a photoelectric eye that automatically turns lights on at dusk and off at dawn, or motion detectors that turn the lights on when someone approaches them.

Low-Voltage Lighting

Lights using only 12 volts of electricity are popular for gardens because they are inexpensive to operate and install. Few code restrictions apply, wiring doesn't always need to be

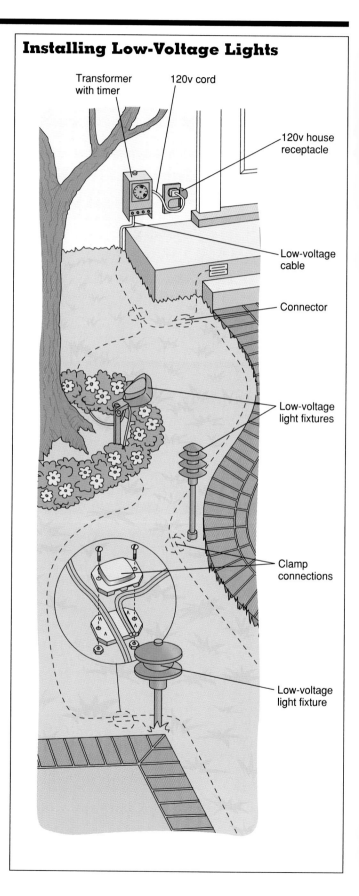

Installing Low-Voltage Lights

Transformer with timer

120v cord

120v house receptacle

Low-voltage cable

Connector

Low-voltage light fixtures

Clamp connections

Low-voltage light fixture

buried, and metal or PVC conduit is unnecessary. Installation is fairly simple. The manufacturer's instructions usually call for mounting the transformer near a standard electrical outlet in the garage, house, or outdoors. Next, attach the low-voltage cable to the terminal screws of the transformer and run it to where you want the light fixtures. Assemble each fixture and snap it to the cable. Insert the support stake for the fixture—do not drive it or you may damage the wire connections. For best results, place lights no more than 100 feet from the transformer. Remember that most low-voltage fixtures use halogen bulbs: Do not touch them with bare hands, because the oily residue your fingers will leave on the bulb will cause it to burn out quickly. Handle halogen bulbs with gloves or tissue paper.

Maintaining Outdoor Structures

Because they are constantly exposed to the elements, outdoor structures can deteriorate quickly if they are not maintained. Keeping the yard clean will be a great help in keeping structures in repair. Remove all leaves, grass, and other yard debris that can build up in corners of your deck or against a fence, trapping moisture that can cause rot and decay. Inspect wood structures at least twice a year, in the spring and fall. Test for rot, especially near the ground, by probing suspicious areas with

a screwdriver. Repair loose boards by removing old nails and reattaching the boards with galvanized deck screws. Check all masonry for chips and missing pieces. Fill all cracks and holes with mortar so water can't cause damage during the winter, when freezing and thawing cycles can cause further deterioration.

Protective Finishes for Wood

Wood is vulnerable to weather, ultraviolet sunlight, wood-destroying insects, mold, mildew, and wear. Nothing can protect wood permanently, but a preservative, sealer, stain, or paint will slow deterioration. Each has advantages and disadvantages. Your choice will depend on the species of lumber, local weather conditions, and desired appearance. Check the manufacturer's recommendations about application, disposal, and effects on plants and animals. Don't apply finishes to new wood, including pressure-treated lumber, until it has weathered for at least two months.

Preservatives

A preservative, which soaks into the wood, resists decay and insects but does not repel water or preserve the color of wood. The most effective form of preservative is applied under pressure, at a factory. For home application, a relatively safe and environmentally acceptable preservative is copper naphthenate. A water-

borne preservative, which is less effective but safer because it emits fewer volatile organic compounds (VOCs), is propynyl butyl carbamate. Wood treated with preservatives should be coated with a sealer, stain, or paint.

Sealers

These chemicals prevent wood from absorbing moisture and delay color changes due to weathering. Don't use a sealer on previously stained or painted surfaces. Some sealers include preservatives, and some may be added to stains or paints. Some absorb ultraviolet light—these provide extra protection against sun bleaching. For decks and stairs, avoid sealers that form hard surfaces that can become slippery.

Stains and Paint

The purpose of a stain, which penetrates into the wood, is to protect it from moisture and add color. Semitransparent, or light-bodied, stains allow the wood grain and texture to show through. They are an appropriate choice for deck and stair surfaces; these stains will make worn areas less noticeable. Solid, or full-bodied, stains hide the grain and knots and are more durable than semitransparent stains. Always choose a nonchalking, or sealer, type of stain.

Paint, although more expensive than other finishes, is ideal for refinishing older structures or low grades of wood. Once you use it, however, there is no other way to maintain or refinish the wood except to repaint it.

Protection Against Mildew

Wood mildew, an early stage of rot, occurs where wood is in prolonged contact with water—for example, when a gutter continues to drip onto a deck long after rain ends. To solve such a problem, repair the source of the moisture and clean the wood with a mixture of water and bleach or a mixture of water and trisodium phosphate (TSP). After it dries reapply wood preservative.

Care of Masonry and Concrete

Masonry is susceptible to stains and organic growth, such as moss. These problems can often be traced to a related water condition. Try to fix the condition that caused the problem. Masonry is also prone to efflorescence, a whitish powdery stain formed when water-soluble salts are washed to the surface. Remove the stain by wire-brushing or apply a solution that will neutralize the salts. Such solutions are available from a masonry supplier. To remove stains caused by dripping or rubbing, apply an industrial abrasive, or pumice and rottenstone. Rub hard with a wire brush dipped in water. To remove moss, clean the stone with a fungicide, according to directions.

Sometimes small chunks of concrete pop away from the surface, a condition called spalling. To correct the problem, chip away all loose concrete, moisten the area, and apply commercial patching compound. Undercut the edges to improve adhesion.

PRIVACY AND ACCESS

The first structures built in a landscaping project are the fences and garden walls needed for creating privacy and defining the property. Right behind them in importance are any gates, walks, paths, steps, and driveways required for easy access around the yard. Even if you don't plan on building any other garden structures, you will probably need to undertake at least one or two projects for privacy or access.

This chapter presents design ideas and construction techniques for meeting both of these fundamental needs. For privacy, you will learn techniques for designing and building fences that are both durable and beautiful. You will learn about the timeless appeal of garden walls and what is involved in building them. For access, you will learn how to enhance your garden with walks, paths, steps, and driveways that are safe, convenient, and decorative.

Few projects offer more return with less effort than an attractive fence and gate. They enhance the property of the owner and can also beautify the neighborhood.

CREATING PRIVACY

We all like to have a place where we can relax and not feel on display. If every time you sit in your backyard you wind up having to wave at and greet your neighbors, then it's time for you to plan a way to have some privacy.

Some Principles of Privacy

To create privacy and a sense of security, you must block some views and enclose the space. This can be done not only around the perimeter of your property, but also around different areas of your yard that you want to define and separate from others. You might, for instance, have a 6-foot-high wood stockade fence and arborvitae around the perimeter and a trellis fence with vines like morning glory or clematis to screen a utility area.

If you live in the city, where backyards are narrow and tall houses are sandwiched together, fences won't provide privacy from above. One solution is an overhead lattice supported on a framework of posts and joists.

Fences

Fences can define boundaries, help control traffic flow in the front yard, and provide privacy in the backyard. Traffic-flow controls (which might be masonry walls) can be any design element that channels people to entrances or prevents them from walking across the yard or cutting corners. Traffic fences, such as post-and-rail or picket fences,

are usually open in design and no more than 2 to 4 feet high.

Privacy fences, such as stockades, are usually about 6 feet high. Many communities have zoning laws prohibiting fences above that level, and some require you to have a permit before erecting one. Check with the local building inspection department about fence regulations.

If you are planning a backyard privacy fence, one of the first things to do is to look at what others in your neighborhood have done. If the norm is a standard 6-foot stockade fence, then don't deviate and make your property stand out by putting up a lattice fence. In addition, make sure you let your neighbors know what you are doing. Although you have the right to put on your property whatever fence you choose (providing it conforms to local zoning laws), etiquette requires that you at least inform your neighbors. Talking with neighbors could pay off: You might be able to split the cost of the fence or share the building effort. And don't forget that it's polite, when you build a fence, to face the finished side toward the neighbor.

Your choice of fence style will depend on several factors.

•Compatibility with the neighborhood and adjacent

Check Your Property Lines

Before installing any fence, locate your property's boundary lines. Putting your fence on your neighbor's property creates ill will, could produce a lawsuit, and might cause trouble at the time of sale.

First, examine your property survey, if you have one. (If you don't, have a survey done and have the surveyor leave stakes showing the lot corners.) Look for a surveyor's marker to use as a corner guide. Using a 100-foot tape measure and a helper, measure from your house and

any other fixed structure to set the lines.

Once you've figured your boundaries, mark them with stakes, set up batter boards, and install a string line. Next, ask your neighbors if they have a survey against which you can check the lot lines you have in common. This will allow you to double-check your measurements. If you're off by an inch, that's probably OK. If you're off by 6 inches, then you need to figure out where the error is.

properties: Use materials, details, and proportions that blend with your house, streetscape elements, and plants.

•Scale: The fence should be neither too large nor too small. Large fences can be made to look smaller by the use of textures and shadow lines and by adjusting the spacing of posts, panels, rails, and caps.

•Proportion and mass: Fences can look awkward if elements are out of balance. For example, a fence with a solid base and a lattice near the top seems right because the base is grounded and the top looks light and airy. However, if the elements are reversed or out of proportion with each other, the fence might seem top-heavy or off balance. In designing, pay attention to the relationship between the height and width of the panels, the size of posts in relation to the fencing material, and the alignment of posts with major horizontal or vertical elements nearby.

•Cost: Factors affecting the cost of a fence are the materials used, fence length, type of detailing, and the skill and labor necessary to erect it. Long-term maintenance costs should also be considered. Brick and metal are more expensive initially but cheaper to maintain and have a much longer life span than wood.

•Likelihood of graffiti: Unfortunately, a fence or wall that faces a street or sidewalk may become a canvas for a graffitist. Discourage graffiti by choosing a fence or wall with no flat surfaces. Remove or paint over defacement as soon as it appears. Products for removing graffiti are similar to paint removers but not as strong. Graffiti removers are less effective on absorbent surfaces, such as brick and unfinished wood, than on smooth surfaces. A painted fence or wall is easier to clean than an unpainted one, and you can always keep extra paint handy for touch-ups.

An iron fence provides security without masking the view.

A white picket fence is traditional and timeless.

White paint gives this rustic rail fence a smart, crisp look.

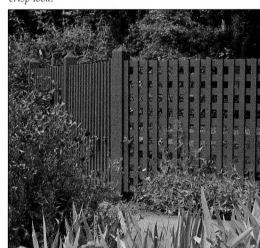

Staggered tops and stepped rails make this board fence distinctive.

Lattice is an effective way to finish the top of a fence.

This fence encloses the garden without blocking the view.

Grooved boards and sweeping curves make an elegant fence.

This black chain link fence blends into the background.

A fence with contrasting colors adds a touch of formality to this entry.

Wood Fences

Probably one of the easiest projects to build is a wooden fence. Construction is usually a straightforward process of setting posts, building the framework, and adding the screening or panels. Be sure to plan the location of any gates and make allowances for posts and alignment.

Because wood fences vary so greatly in style and quality, cost is likewise variable. If you are hiring someone to supply materials and build the fence, the bid will be the cost estimate. If you will do the work yourself, you can do a quick materials estimate by pricing fence packages at a lumberyard or home center. These packages, which include the posts, framing lumber, and fencing material, are priced by the lineal foot of finished fence; just multiply the lineal-foot cost by the total length of fence you will need. Find out if the package price includes delivery, concrete, nails, hardware, and stain or preservative, and adjust your estimate accordingly. The resulting estimate represents the low end of the range of cost options. To control costs, you have several options. One is to modify the design to conserve materials or to utilize labor more efficiently. If the fence is extremely simple, you might find it worthwhile to hire an experienced crew who could build it in a couple of days. On the other hand, if you are building the fence yourself and have the time, you might consider a more intricate design since labor is free.

The quality of materials also affects cost, and quality can vary widely. In comparing costs, be sure to examine the materials themselves. If using natural woods, such as redwood and cedar, be wary of lumber with a high percentage of sapwood and few growth rings per inch (examine the wood in cross section, by looking at the end of the board). Rough, unsurfaced lumber is less expensive than surfaced lumber and is suitable for designs that have a rustic style. If using pressure-treated lumber, be sure that posts are specified for ground contact and that defects in all the lumber are at a minimum—pressure-treated lumber is usually of lower grade. The price of pressure-treated lumber may be affected by color (greenish, brownish, or reddish); whether boards have incisement marks; and whether lumber is kiln-dried after treatment (KDAT). Kiln drying ensures straighter boards and, usually, a higher price. If price prevents you from using top-grade lumber throughout your fence, the posts, rails, and stringers, at least, should be the most durable and stable that you can afford.

Setting the Posts

Most fence posts are 4×4s, but unsupported corners and posts for heavy gates should be 6×6 or larger. To build the fence, start with the groundwork, which consists of clearing away any existing fence and vegetation, laying out string lines, and digging the holes. To align posts, stretch a string line between batter boards. To establish the position of each posthole, divide the distance between corner posts into equal spaces—set most posts 4 to 8 feet apart, depending how far the horizontal fence members can span without sagging. Dig the holes with an auger or clamshell digger—shovels make the holes too large. Depths vary, but minimums are 18 inches for 4-foot fences, 24 inches for 6-foot fences, and 36 inches for 6×6 gateposts and end posts.

Fill the bottom of each hole with 4 to 6 inches of rock or gravel. Set the corner posts first. Plumb them with a level,

There are many ways to work lattice panels into a fence. Here, horizontal placement with a dividing rail close to the ground reduces the impact of the fence's height.

Aligning Fence Posts

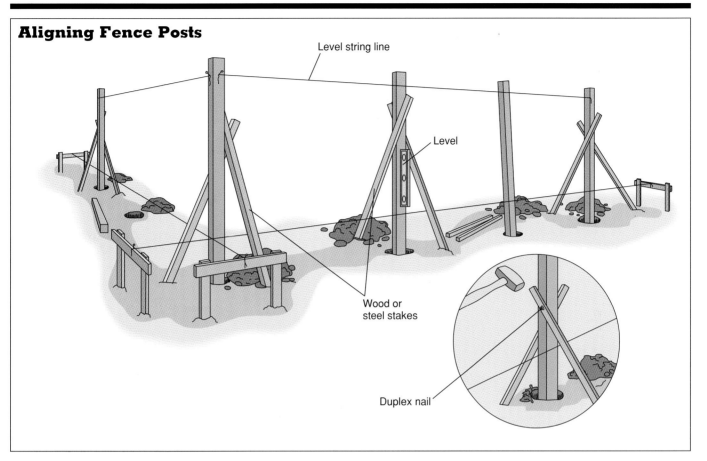

Level string line

Level

Wood or
steel stakes

Duplex nail

Setting Posts

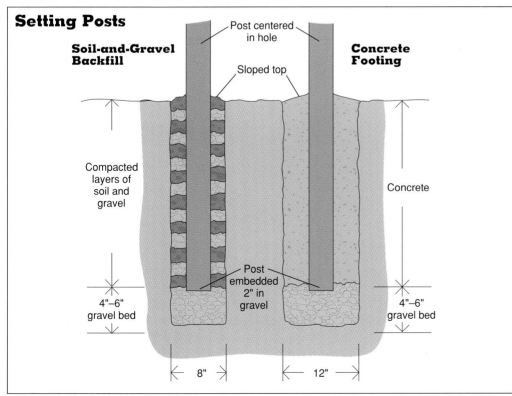

**Soil-and-Gravel
Backfill**

**Concrete
Footing**

Post centered
in hole

Sloped top

Compacted
layers of
soil and
gravel

Concrete

Post
embedded
2" in
gravel

4"–6"
gravel bed

4"–6"
gravel bed

8"

12"

align them with the string line, and brace them diagonally in both directions. Stretch another string, above the first, between post tops. Align the rest of the posts to the upper and lower string lines, bracing each post in two directions.

In mild-winter areas, backfill the postholes with concrete. In heavy-frost areas where soils are firm and stable, backfill with alternating layers of gravel and soil to reduce displacement from frost heaves. Or pour a foot of concrete around the bottom of each post, add a layer of gravel, and fill the top 6 inches of the hole with concrete. Then slide a tapered shingle between each side of the post and the concrete to form an

Building on a Slope

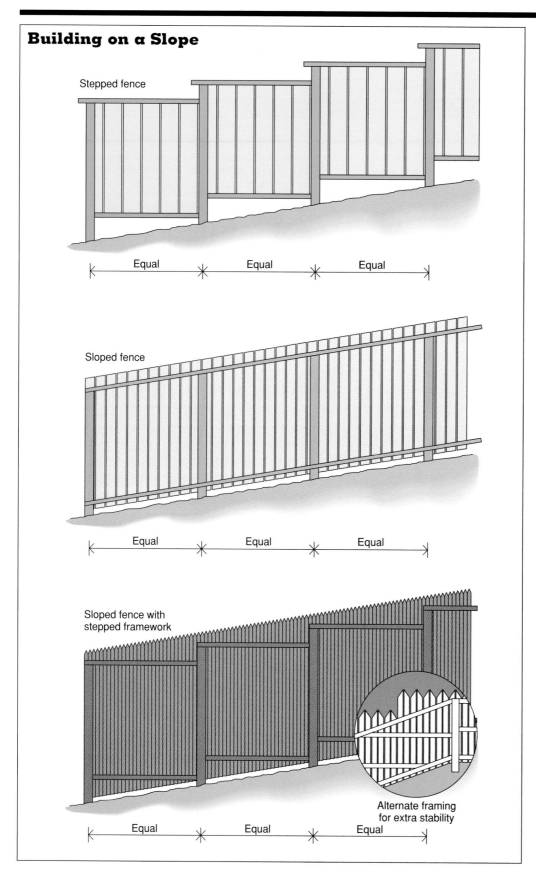

Stepped fence

| Equal | Equal | Equal |

Sloped fence

| Equal | Equal | Equal |

Sloped fence with stepped framework

Alternate framing for extra stability

| Equal | Equal | Equal |

expansion gap. After the concrete sets, remove the shingles and fill the gaps with tar or roofing caulk. If the soil is not firm, use a 12-inch-diameter forming tube to stabilize the hole sides while you pour the concrete and gravel.

Building the Frame

Wait at least 24 hours for the concrete to set. Then, mark and cut the post tops. The height will vary with the fence design—whether the fence boards extend above the top rail or are framed by it—and ground conditions. If building on a slope, you'll have to decide between a stepped fence, a sloped fence, or a sloped fence with stepped framework. To level a fence, use a water level, builder's level, or long straightedge and a carpenter's level to align the cutting marks.

After cutting the posts, attach the top rails. Use 2×4s long enough to span two or three bays, and locate all joints over posts. Predrill before nailing the ends of boards; drive two 16-penny (16d) galvanized nails into each 2×4 at each post and four nails at joints. For extra stability and an attractive shadow line, nail a 2×6 cap rail over the top rail, staggering the joints.

Cut 2×4 bottom rails to fit between the posts. To keep them level, measure from the top rail, not the ground. Toenail them to the fence posts with 16d galvanized screw nails; predrill first. To keep the fence from sagging between posts and to control weeds and small animals, install a 1-by board of pressure-treated lumber, set on edge, under the

Installing Rails, Stringers, and Kickboards

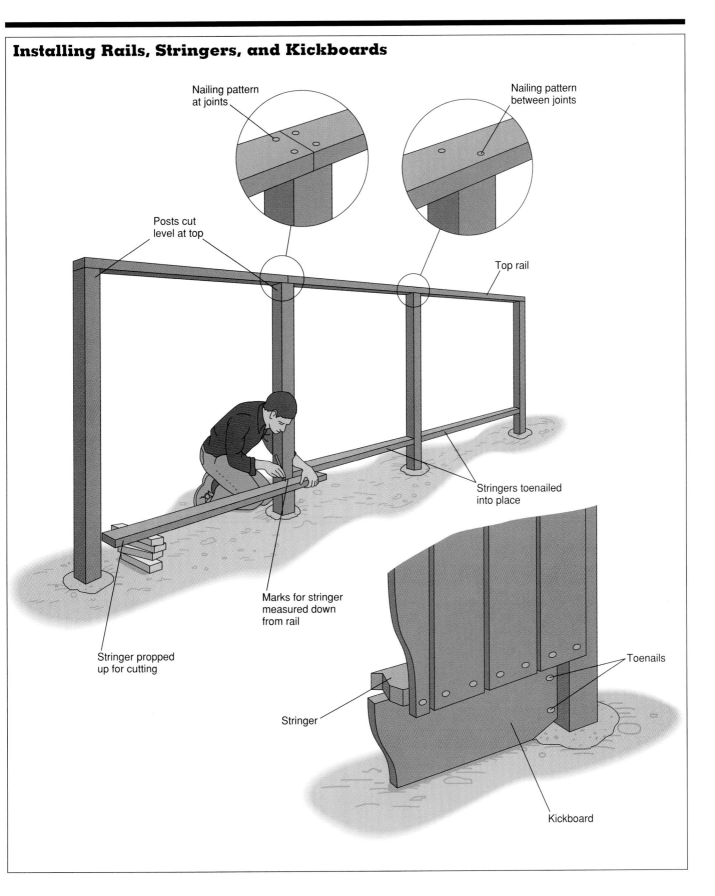

Nailing pattern at joints

Nailing pattern between joints

Posts cut level at top

Top rail

Stringers toenailed into place

Marks for stringer measured down from rail

Stringer propped up for cutting

Toenails

Stringer

Kickboard

2×4 rails. This 1-by, called a kickboard, should rest on the ground; you may have to trim the board or dig away soil to get it to fit. Toenail it to the posts and rails, predrilling first. The kickboard will eventually rot, but it is much easier to replace than dozens of vertical fence members that rest directly on the ground.

Completing the Fence

Once the framework is in place, attaching the fence boards, lattice, or other panels to the framework is monotonous but easy work. For a long fence, especially if boards will be toenailed, rent a pneumatic nailing gun and compressor to speed the process. Make sure the nails are galvanized. Near the edges of boards, predrill holes for nails, and use a level from time to time to check the vertical alignment of boards. If the tops extend above the top rail, use a level string line to keep the tops aligned. If the design calls for gaps between boards, ensure uniform spacing by using as a spacer a scrap of wood long enough to cover both rails.

Let the wood season for a few weeks, then finish the fence with a sealer, stain, or paint (see page 29).

Metal Fences

Ornamental iron and wrought iron fences are usually placed in the front of a house to define perimeter and channel traffic. They can enhance security, but they provide no visual privacy. Ornamental iron fences require just the right setting to produce a desirable effect. An iron fence in front of a stone townhouse can look sophisticated; the same fence on a suburban lawn in front of a Cape Cod house is unattractively out of place. Ornamental fences should usually be designed and fabricated by a professional—local artisans may be able to create a work of art. Do-it-yourself kits are available from home improvement centers, but before you buy, compare the sturdiness of the product with that of a custom-built fence.

Scrap-iron dealers and salvage yards that specialize in fixtures from old houses are sources of used ornamental fences. Magazines for home renovators may give you a lead on other sources. If you are able to locate a fence you like and it's long enough, then you'll need to do the following.

• Arrange transportation: Either have the fence delivered or rent a trailer.

• Clean the fence: Sandblasting is the best way to remove rust and paint. You can rent the equipment and do it yourself or have a professional sandblaster do it for you.

• Paint the fence: You'll need to give it a thorough prime coat and one or two finish coats. Use an oil-based paint formulated for rust prevention. The easiest course is usually to paint the fence before installation—lay it, one section at a time, on two sawhorses; paint one side; then turn it over.

• Install the fence: To be sturdy, an iron fence needs a continuous concrete footing or a short brick wall as a base. If you pour a footing, set the anchors that are provided on the bases of the fence sections within the forms, which have been aligned with string lines. Brace each anchor, post, or fence section so it doesn't move. Pour the concrete, finish the footing, and let it cure for seven days. Keep the surface moist or cover it with plastic while the concrete cures.

In contrast to ornamental fences, chain link fences are strictly utilitarian and are best used for building dog kennels and the like. Very durable and functional, they don't contribute to any design and afford no privacy. Even when metal or wood slats have been inserted in the links or when the links are coated with vinyl, a chain link fence brings the look of a prison to a property. If you need a chain link fence for security, consider a 6-foot chain link installation with small links (small links are harder to climb than large ones) that has a wood stockade fence of equal height attached to the inside.

A screen of vertical lattice panels creates separate areas—public and private—in this yard.

Privacy Screens

A privacy screen added to a deck or installed in the yard sets off the area and can provide shade. A simple and effective material for privacy screens, and one sold in most lumberyards and home centers, is prefabricated 4×8 lattice. Lattice panels may be made from redwood, cedar, pressure-treated wood, or vinyl. Be careful what you buy. The lath in some lattice is too thin or contains a large amount of sapwood, and the staples holding it together are flimsy. Compare before you purchase.

Like lumber, lattice comes in grades.

•Clear grade: The best on the market. Wood is clear sawn, smooth, and virtually flawless. Panels contain very little sapwood.

•No. 1 and better grade: Contains a high percentage of clear lath with some sound knots and other minor wood defects.

•Select standard and better grade: This is structurally sound lattice, but it contains more knots and machine-torn and rough-sawn edges than do higher grades.

Vinyl lattice, made from polyvinyl chloride (PVC) plastic, has a surface finish that looks like fine grainless wood with a coat of satin paint. Vinyl lattice won't rot and has no grain to split. It can be installed in direct contact with the ground.

Building a privacy screen using lattice is similar to erecting a fence. Sometimes lattice can be nailed directly to posts sunk in the ground. A better way is to install it in a frame.

The parts for this may be sold at the same place you buy the lattice.

The final touch to latticework are lovely vines that grow on it. If you want to use latticework for a trellis or overhead, build it with 1×2s to provide the stability required.

Walls

Garden walls can be used to create privacy, define boundaries, provide seating, create attractive backdrops, retain a slope, deflect sound, screen out wind, or establish planting beds. Your design will depend on how many of these things you want your wall to do. Design factors include decisions about materials, height, structural configuration, and plantings that will complement the wall.

A low garden wall (6 to 12 inches) can be a visual boundary and can also divide your garden into areas for different uses. A higher wall (17 to 21 inches), topped with a stone slab or wood bench, can serve as a seat for relaxing and admiring the garden.

A masonry wall may be just a few courses high to mark the edge of a lawn. Or it can be a curving brick enclosure, built by a master mason, that surrounds an estate—the kind of wall beyond the scope of this book and one that would certainly exceed most budgets! Walls lower than 3 feet are suitable do-it-yourself projects.

Choosing Materials

Since a wall is relatively permanent, consider carefully how it will blend with your yard before you choose materials. You will want something tasteful and appropriate to your home. The scale of the wall and materials must be in balance with the scale of the garden and size of the yard. Visit several masonry yards in your area and compare brick, concrete block, local stone, and manufactured stone. Also take a look at timber.

Brick and concrete blocks are modular units that create a strong grid pattern unless they are covered with a cement or stucco veneer, called parging. Because bricks are smaller than concrete blocks, the grid has a softer, more textured effect. The red of brick complements greenery.

Stone is a fundamental building material, in use for thousands of years. A stone

Building a Privacy Screen

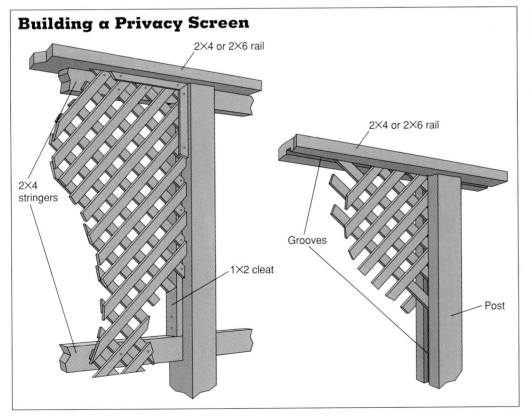

2×4 or 2×6 rail

2×4 stringers

1×2 cleat

2×4 or 2×6 rail

Grooves

Post

wall evokes a sense of permanence; it can look either rustic or refined. You can build a dry stone wall (which doesn't need a footing) or a mortared stone wall. Of the many variations on the basic stone wall are walls that include broken concrete and those with stone veneers applied to poured concrete or concrete block.

If you are overwhelmed by the choices (and that can happen), take some photos of your home with you and get opinions from knowledgeable sales staff.

In addition to the aesthetic qualities of materials, also consider ease of construction. A wall of stacked landscaping timbers, although more appropriate for retaining walls than

for decorative garden walls, is the easiest to build. Building a dry stone wall is also relatively easy. Mortaring stone requires more work. Working with concrete block demands less patience than building a dry stone wall but more precision. Brickwork, because of the small units involved and the meticulousness required to achieve the desired formal effect, is the most difficult. If you want the look of a mortared stone or brick wall, you may be able to cut your material cost and time by using concrete block for the wall and then facing it with brick, flagstone, rock, or manufactured stone. This requires correct use of mortar to adhere the facing material to the block

and simultaneously tie the facing units together. Block alone doesn't make a very attractive wall, although the effect can be improved by covering it with stucco parging or using decorative concrete block, such as slump blocks or split-face blocks.

Wall-Building Basics

Except for dry stone walls and wood walls, all garden walls should be supported by a concrete footing. The width and thickness of the footing depend on the size of the wall, and the depth depends on local soil conditions and the frost line. Most footings are twice as wide as the width of the wall; the footing width

for a retaining wall is usually two-thirds the height of the wall. The footing should be at least 8 inches thick for low walls. For walls over 2 feet high, construct a 12-inch-thick footing. For higher walls, consult an engineer or qualified masonry contractor.

A footing should have a 6-inch layer of gravel beneath it to absorb the heaving from unstable soil or deep frosts. In areas with heavy freezing, excavate the trench deep enough for the gravel to lie below the frost line.

Footings should have horizontal steel reinforcement to help prevent cracking. Two lengths of ½-inch (No. 4) rebar is usually sufficient for low walls. To tie the wall to the footing, set anchor bolts or short lengths of vertical rebar into the footing concrete, spaced so the wall materials will fit around them.

Dry Stone Walls

To build a dry, or loose-laid, stone wall, you first need to select the type of stone you want (usually a flat kind, since you'll be stacking them one on top of another). Figure out how high, wide, and long your wall will be and take the measurements to the masonry yard. When the stone is delivered, it will probably arrive on pallets with a wire screen holding them in place. The truck delivery could crack the driveway or leave deep ruts in the lawn. You may want to ask the driver to leave the pallets at curbside.

Next, separate the stones by size. Set aside the flattest and broadest, for the top course. In another place put

The stones for this short retaining wall are being set with mortar.

Building a Dry Stone Wall

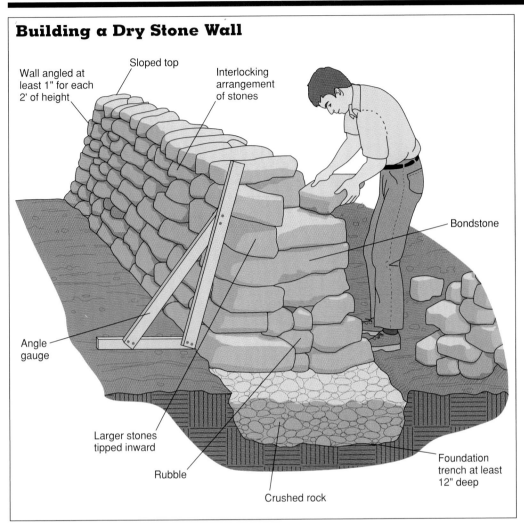

Wall angled at least 1" for each 2' of height

Sloped top

Interlocking arrangement of stones

Bondstone

Angle gauge

Larger stones tipped inward

Rubble

Crushed rock

Foundation trench at least 12" deep

stones wide or long enough to stretch across the width of the wall near the bottom. These bondstones, or headers, stabilize the wall. Using a wheelbarrow and helpers, organize the stones in piles at regular intervals along the site so they will be ready when you build the wall.

Although you won't need a concrete footing, you will have to dig a trench at least 12 inches deep or to just below the frost line. Backfill the trench with compacted crushed rock.

Use batter boards and mason's twine to keep the wall straight as you build it. Build the base wider than the top

and build up the ends before filling in the courses. Try to tilt all stones downward toward the middle. Fill cavities with smaller stones and rubble. Give both faces of the wall a batter (a very slight pyramiding) as you build it. Cap the wall with the large flat stones and tilt them slightly so water can run off.

Mortared Stone Walls

Building a mortared stone wall is similar to building a dry stone wall, except that you will have to construct a concrete footing (see page 25). And, of course, you will be setting the stones in mortar.

Stones with straight sides are the easiest to work with; round fieldstones are the hardest. It is not the mortar that glues the stones together; it is their own weight. So, if the wall isn't set right, you can't rely on the mortar to hold it together. The mortar is important nonetheless, to fill voids and stabilize the stones. Make sure the stones are clean so the mortar will stick.

Mortar for a stone wall should have more cement in it than mortar used in a brick wall, and it should not contain lime, which could stain the stone. Mix 3 parts sand to 1 part portland cement. Add ½

part fireclay for better consistency. The mortar should be dry enough so it balls in your hand but not so dry that it crumbles.

Use stakes or batter boards, and mason's twine, to keep the wall straight as you build it. For the first course, spread a 1-inch layer of mortar over the footing at one end and lay a bondstone. Spread more mortar. Lay large stones along the outside edges of the wall, interspersing them with bondstones every 5 to 6 feet. Fill in the center with small stones, rubble, and mortar.

For remaining courses, do a dry layout to make sure joints are staggered and stones fit. Then lay mortar over the first course and set the stones. If too much mortar oozes out, prop the stone with wood shims and fill the voids. Remove the shims when the mortar sets. Check the sides of the wall often to make sure they are plumb. Batter the wall about 1 inch for every 2 feet in height, unless the walls are stable enough to remain vertical.

Remove excess mortar from stones as quickly as possible, and wash the wall with clear water after all the joints have dried. Soapy water should remove stains. Use a muriatic acid mixture (1 part acid added to 10 parts water) as a last resort.

Another way to build a stone wall is to build a form as if you were pouring a concrete wall. Fill the form with stones and concrete. Work slowly and arrange the stones against the forms, filling the voids with small stones so you won't have wide bands of

Building a Mortared Stone Wall

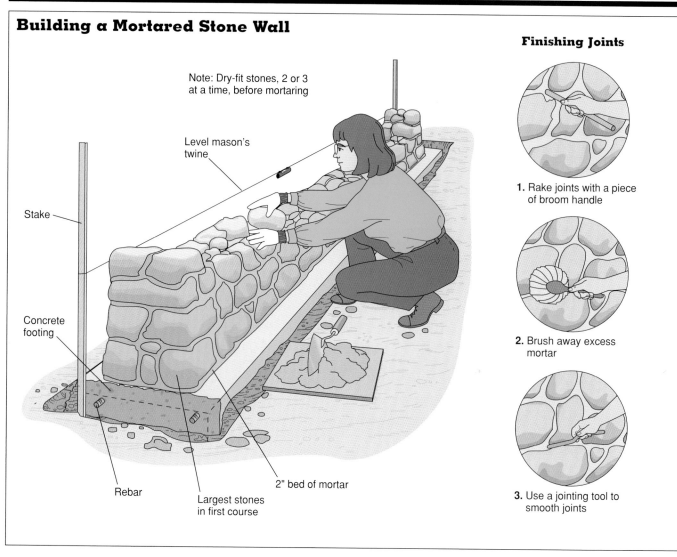

Note: Dry-fit stones, 2 or 3 at a time, before mortaring

Level mason's twine

Stake

Concrete footing

Rebar

Largest stones in first course

2" bed of mortar

Finishing Joints

1. Rake joints with a piece of broom handle

2. Brush away excess mortar

3. Use a jointing tool to smooth joints

---

concrete showing. By filling the interior cavity with concrete and rebar you can build a very strong wall with a smooth stone face.

Concrete Block Walls

The footing of a concrete block wall should be 16 inches wide and 12 inches thick, with vertical rebar spaced every 3 to 4 feet and aligning with the cells of the blocks. To set blocks, lay out a dry run on the footing, with ⅜- to ½-inch spaces between the blocks for the joints. Make alignment marks on the footing for all the joints, take

the blocks off the footing, and locate the two outside corners. Spread a layer of mortar at one end and place the corner block into it, pressing it down to within ⅜ inch of the footing. Lay a block at the other corner in the same way, and stretch a line between them to guide the rest of the first course.

To finish the course, lay mortar on the footing and butter one end of each block before setting it in place. Lay blocks with the web, or wider side, up. As you lay each block, keep the buttered end

raised slightly; then, in one smooth motion, lower it and fit it snugly against the preceding block. Scrape away any excess mortar. Butter both ends of the last block. To finish joints, compress the mortar with a jointing tool, clean off excess mortar, strike (smooth) the joint again, and clean the wall with a dry brush.

As you build up the courses, stagger the joints by starting every other course with a half block. Stretch mason's twine between the corner blocks of each course, and check your work frequently

with a level, both horizontally and vertically. If you intend to veneer the wall with stones or brick, in every other course insert in the mortar metal ties at 2-foot intervals.

If the height of the wall requires longer vertical rebar, wire new pieces to the originals. Lay a bond beam—a row of blocks with cutouts at the ends for horizontal rebar— every fifth course or according to code. After finishing the wall, strike all the joints with a jointing tool or a bent piece of ¾-inch copper pipe. Then fill the cells containing vertical

Building a Concrete Block Wall

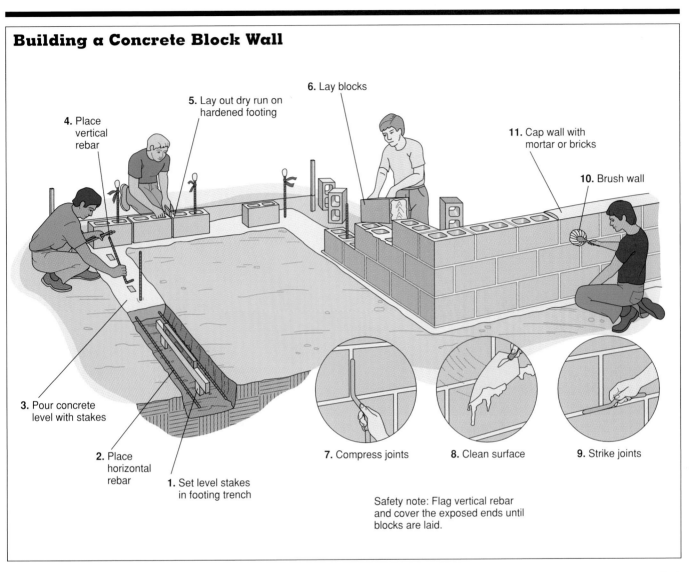

4. Place vertical rebar

5. Lay out dry run on hardened footing

6. Lay blocks

11. Cap wall with mortar or bricks

10. Brush wall

3. Pour concrete level with stakes

2. Place horizontal rebar

1. Set level stakes in footing trench

7. Compress joints

8. Clean surface

9. Strike joints

Safety note: Flag vertical rebar and cover the exposed ends until blocks are laid.

rebar with grout (loose concrete with ⅜-inch aggregate). If you are pouring a cap across the top of the wall, use building paper to keep the grout from falling into the cavities. If you are building a retaining wall, grout the entire wall.

Brick Walls

For stability, a brick wall should be two wythes (rows of bricks) wide. The space between wythes is the thickness of a mortar joint, which makes it possible to span both wythes with a single brick. A brick placed this way, across the wall from front to back, is called a header and the resulting brick pattern is called common bond.

Build a level footing 16 inches wide and at least 8 inches thick. If the wall will step down a sloped site, the height of each step should be a multiple of the thickness of one brick, plus mortar. Finish the footing surface with a wood float; a smooth finish is not necessary. After the concrete hardens, lay the bricks in a ½-inch bed of fresh mortar, working in small sections. Mix mortar in small batches—

enough for about one hour of bricklaying. It should be loose and moist, not runny or stiff. Soak the bricks in water ahead of time. As with concrete blocks, lay the corner blocks first and fill in between them. Joints should be ⅜ to ½ inch wide. When you insert the last brick in each course, called a closure brick, butter the end of the brick already laid and both ends of the closure brick.

As you lay successive courses, instead of completing each course before starting the next, start four or five courses at each end of the wall, result-

ing in two small towers, called leads. Stretch mason's twine from the bottom course of bricks in one lead to the corresponding brick in the other, and fill in the course. Proceed until the wall is filled between both leads, then build new ones and repeat the process. Start alternating courses with headers, or half bricks, unless you prefer a different pattern.

In every fourth course embed metal wall ties into the mortar to bond the two wythes together, especially if you are using a brick pattern that doesn't include headers.

43

Building a Brick Wall

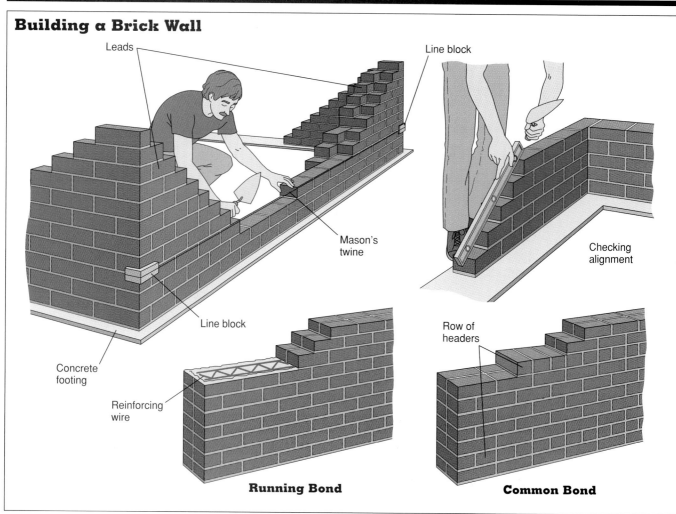

Leads

Line block

Mason's twine

Line block

Concrete footing

Reinforcing wire

Checking alignment

Row of headers

Running Bond

Common Bond

Bricklaying Techniques

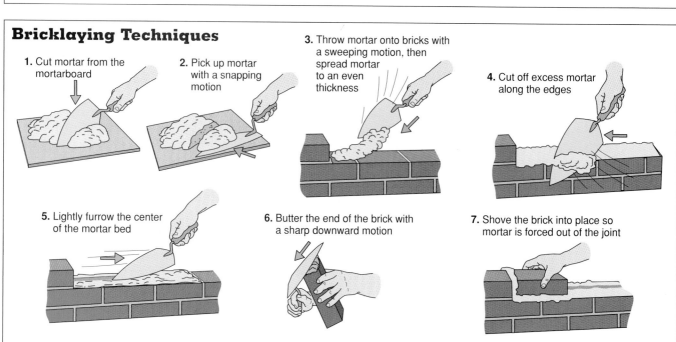

1. Cut mortar from the mortarboard

2. Pick up mortar with a snapping motion

3. Throw mortar onto bricks with a sweeping motion, then spread mortar to an even thickness

4. Cut off excess mortar along the edges

5. Lightly furrow the center of the mortar bed

6. Butter the end of the brick with a sharp downward motion

7. Shove the brick into place so mortar is forced out of the joint

Wall ties are corrugated metal strips and should be spaced 2 to 3 feet apart; stagger them in relation to the ties in previous courses. An optional type of reinforcement is a zigzag strip of galvanized welded wire, which you can cut to fit.

Strike off excess mortar, keeping the bricks clean as you work. Every three or four courses, or after the mortar sets up, smooth and shape the mortar joints with a jointing tool or bent piece of ½-inch copper pipe. Again, clean off all excess mortar. When you finish the wall, sweep away excess mortar and touch up the joints with the tool. After completing the installation, allow the mortar to cure for two days by periodically spraying the joints with a fine mist or by covering the entire wall with a tent of plastic sheeting. (Make sure that the sheeting does not touch the brick.)

Retaining Walls

Retaining walls, which hold back hillsides, have more of a structural and decorative function than a privacy-related function. Because they must resist the weight of the earth that is being retained plus the pressure of the water trapped behind them, they must be designed carefully. Most homeowners should be able to design and build a simple low wall, but any wall over 3 feet high should be engineered and built by professionals.

If you are designing your own retaining wall, keep in mind that water will be the most serious threat to your creation; hydrostatic pressure may force it to buckle. There are two basic ways to relieve water pressure. One is to make holes, called weep holes, along the base of the wall. The other is to lay a drainpipe on the inside base of the wall and cover it with large gravel or drain rock.

To make weep holes in a timber wall, just drill 1-inch holes every 2 feet. To prevent the holes from clogging with dirt, as you're building the wall cover the holes with fiberglass mesh laid against the holes on the inside face of the wall. The mesh will work best if you anchor it with sand

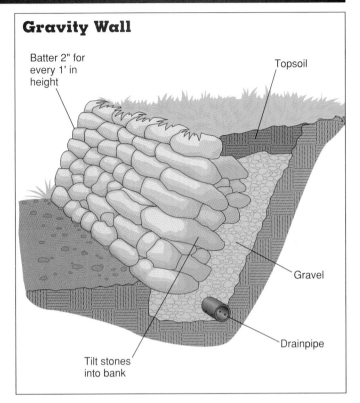

Gravity Wall

Batter 2" for every 1' in height

Topsoil

Gravel

Drainpipe

Tilt stones into bank

A series of short retaining walls eliminates the need to build a single, tall, imposing one. Several short walls also create the opportunity for terraced planting beds.

or gravel outside the holes so the water will be able to trickle out. If you don't want water seeping out from under the wall, install drainpipe (see pages 16 and 17).

Some commonly used types of retaining walls are gravity, cantilevered, green, and timber walls.

Gravity Walls

A gravity wall holds the earth by sheer mass. Usually these walls are low and made of unmortared stone. The base is wider than the top. The visible face of the wall is battered and the earth side is vertical.

Cantilevered Walls

A cantilevered wall consists of a horizontal base and a vertical stem wall that are securely tied together. These are usually used on larger projects and should be designed by a structural engineer. They can be built of concrete or block with rebar in the footing and to tie in the wall. The depth of the footing should be at least one-third the height of the wall or to just below the frost line, whichever is deeper. The width of the footing should be 0.6 times the height. The vertical face can be finished with brick or stone veneer.

Green Walls

These walls combine vegetation and precast interlocking block filled with soil. The units are set in a staggered arrangement, each unit resting on the one beneath it. Green walls can be set against the angle of incline.

Timber Walls

If the wall is to be less than 3 feet high, timber may be appropriate. Timbers can be stacked horizontally, or embedded vertically into the ground. To keep the wall from overturning, at least half the height must be below grade. Stacked timbers are tied together with ½-inch galvanized steel bars driven through undersized holes. Timbers are either pressure-treated 6×6s or railroad ties. Stagger joints to permit weep holes, which were discussed earlier in this chapter. One way to stabilize a timber wall is to set horizontal timbers, called deadmen, into the earth at a right angle to the wall and intersecting it.

Cantilevered Wall

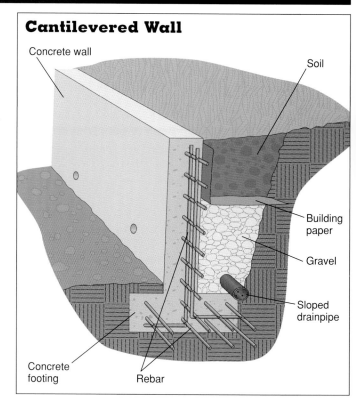

Concrete wall

Soil

Building paper

Gravel

Sloped drainpipe

Concrete footing

Rebar

Green Wall

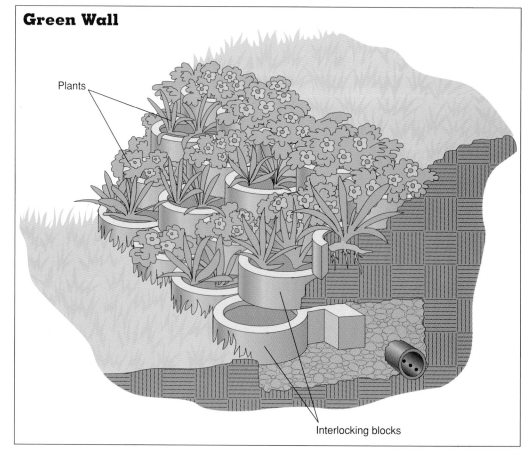

Plants

Interlocking blocks

Timber Wall

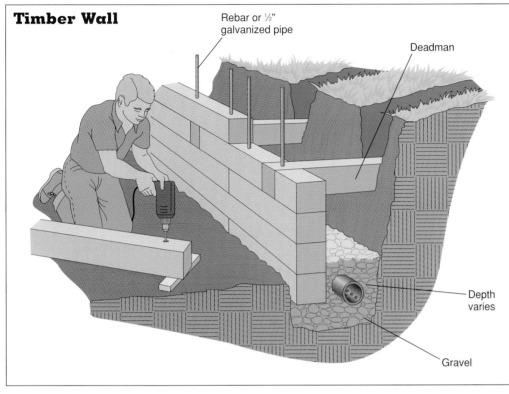

Rebar or ½" galvanized pipe

Deadman

Depth varies

Gravel

Berms

Berms are small, elongated artificial hills. Depending on the size of the lot and scale of the berm, you can construct a berm that, with the addition of screen plantings, can increase privacy, deflect wind, and help reduce street noise. Berms can be edged with low stone or timber walls or planted with grass. Mowing is easier if the slope of the berm is no steeper than 1:3 (1 foot of elevation for every 3 feet of horizontal distance). Because of the volume of dirt involved, rent a small landscaping tractor. Have the topsoil supplier figure out how much fill you will need. You can reduce the amount of topsoil needed by using rubble for the base, or core, of the berm.

This berm, high enough to block views, has been in place long enough for trees to establish themselves.

PROVIDING ACCESS

Welcome. That's what access is all about, whether it be an inviting walk, a gate, a garden patch encouraging discovery, or a convenient place to park. In this section you will learn how to design and build gates, paths, walks, and steps. It also presents options to consider in designing a driveway.

Gates

A gate, especially a well-designed one, says something about the homeowners. Put thought into your gate so that it speaks well of you.

Design Options

Gates need not be the same material as the fence or wall. For example, a wood stockade fence with fieldstone posts (built around a core of concrete blocks) and an antique iron gate salvaged from a demolition site could be a handsome local attraction.

To develop a design, look at as many gates as possible: big gates, small gates, gates from mansions, gates in front of brownstones, and gates for suburban homes. If you have gates in a backyard fence, you may want to use the same style for the front yard, but in proper scale. A backyard gate is usually 6 feet high and 3 to 4 feet wide. A front yard gate is usually low, about 40 to 48 inches, but wider than a backyard gate. Use a double gate for openings wider than 4 feet. Always have the gate swing into your property, or hinge it so it can swing both ways. A wide variety of gate hardware, from hinges to latches, is available. Choose fixtures that match the style of your gate.

Construction

Even if you hire someone to build the fence or wall, you might enjoy reserving gate construction for yourself, especially if you relish a chance for creativity and artistic flair. Choose high-grade lumber—clear, if possible—unless you plan to paint the gate.

Providing Support Posts

For strength and appearance, make gateposts larger than fence posts—ideally, twice the size. For example, if 4×4s were used in the run, use 8×8s for the two gateposts. Or, as an alternative to gateposts, build concrete block columns with brick or stone veneer. The column will have to be at least as high as the fence and capped with a flat stone. As you build the column, embed hanger bolts in the mortar for the top and bottom gate hinges and the latch. Use a level to ensure that the hinge bolts are plumb.

Building the Gate

Measure the opening at the top and bottom. Allow ½ inch on each side of the gate for clearance. A simple 2×4 box

This gate is distinguished from the fence by its posts, the curve in the upper edge of the pickets, and the solid panels at the bottom.

Careful attention to detail—the pedimental top and applied moldings—gives this lattice gate a somewhat formal, architectural quality.

Gate Construction

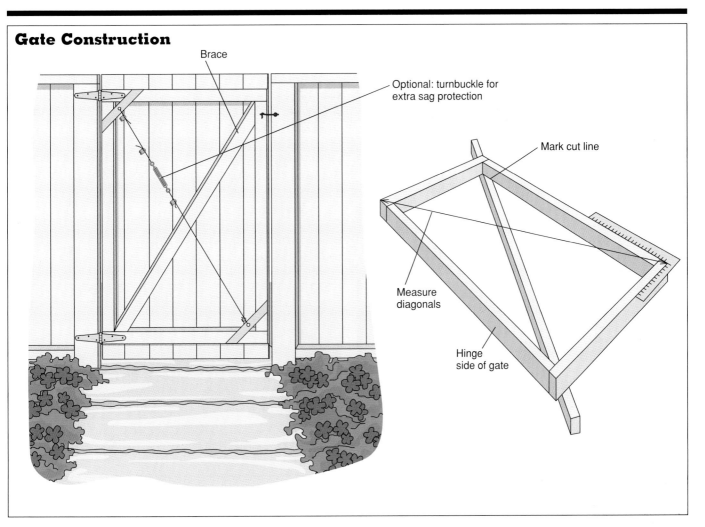

Brace

Optional: turnbuckle for extra sag protection

Mark cut line

Measure diagonals

Hinge side of gate

frame with a diagonal "Z" brace is the basic frame for many designs. To build it, cut the top and bottom pieces to the width of the opening, less 1 inch for clearance. Attach the side pieces between them with two 16d galvanized twist nails or two 4-inch galvanized deck screws at each joint; predrill to prevent splitting. To mark the diagonal 2×4 for cutting, lay it in place over (or under) the box frame, with one end at the corner of the frame where the lower hinge will be installed. See if the frame is square by measuring between opposite corners; the diagonal dimensions should be equal. Then

center the brace over each corner, scribe where it intersects the frame, and cut at these marks to form the angled points at each end of the brace. Drill pilot holes in the frame members and nail or screw the brace in place. Test-fit the frame in the gate opening and decide how the hinges should be mounted so the gate will be flush with the fence face and swing the right way.

Attach the fence boards, lattice, or decorative boards to the frame as the design requires, predrilling and then inserting galvanized screws. Attach heavy-duty hinges to the gate, positioning them so screws or bolts will go into the frame.

The knuckles should be centered about ¼ inch outside the gate, in perfect vertical alignment with each other. Set the gate in the opening so it has equal clearance all around; use blocks to steady it. Attach each hinge to the post with one or two screws, test the swing, and install the rest of the screws. Attach the latch last.

Walks and Paths

If an open gate is an invitation to come onto your property, then walks and paths guide those who enter. That's the purpose of a walk—to direct traffic.

A walk need not be a straight no-nonsense corridor. It can meander. It should relate well to the grounds. It may provide visual interest, following a line such as a retaining wall or directing attention to a flower bed or an attractive tree.

In laying out walks and paths, take a close look at the terrain. If a dip in the ground collects water, fill it in or provide a drain. In addition to keeping your feet dry, the improvement may prevent injury to—and even lawsuits from—people who slip on mud or ice.

If the topography of the grounds is irregular, then consider how you will get from one level to another. You may be able to build a path that follows the contours of the land, if you have enough room. Otherwise, you will need to build some steps.

If you don't already have a walk and are just in the planning stages, wait. Observe people's traffic patterns and let them "vote with their feet" for the pathways that will meet the most needs. After the voting clarifies where the walk is needed, you must choose the material from which to build it.

Materials

The character of a walk or path depends on the materials used to build it. Your choices are concrete, brick, paving stone, flagstone, gravel, crushed stone, tile, and wood chips. For a formal walk, from the sidewalk to the house, concrete or mortared brick is usually used, but brick or interlocking pavers set in sand, or flagstone or cut bluestone set in mortar will also work nicely. The goal is to provide firm, solid footing, and if you live in snow country, be sure the walk is smooth enough for easy shoveling. In the backyard you may want something informal. A crushed-stone path in the garden, flagstones set in grass, or even wood chips contained by wood or timber edging are common choices.

Edgings

Another element for you to consider as you plan a walk is the type of edging it will have. An edging sets off a walk and helps define it. Common edging materials are pressure-treated timbers or planks, brick, and stone—materials that work well as edgings for garden beds too.

Plantings will eventually fill in around this flagstone path; the informal style eliminates the need for straight edges and tedious stonecutting.

The pattern used for this brick walk, which is called basket weave, creates a uniform, serene texture.

Building a Brick-in-Sand Walk

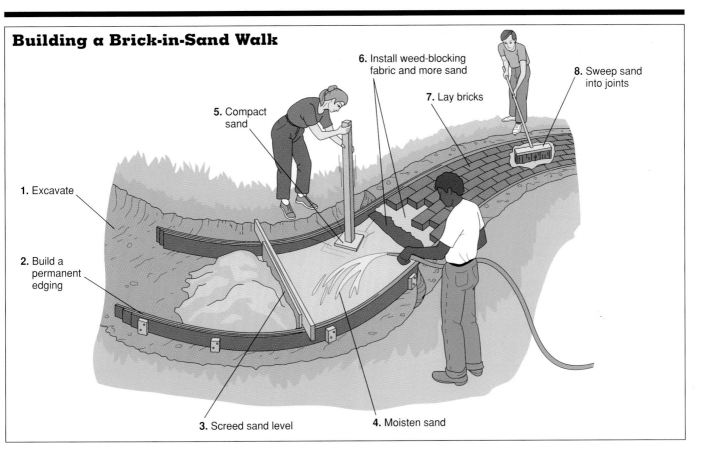

5. Compact sand

6. Install weed-blocking fabric and more sand

7. Lay bricks

8. Sweep sand into joints

1. Excavate

2. Build a permanent edging

3. Screed sand level

4. Moisten sand

Building a Concrete Walk

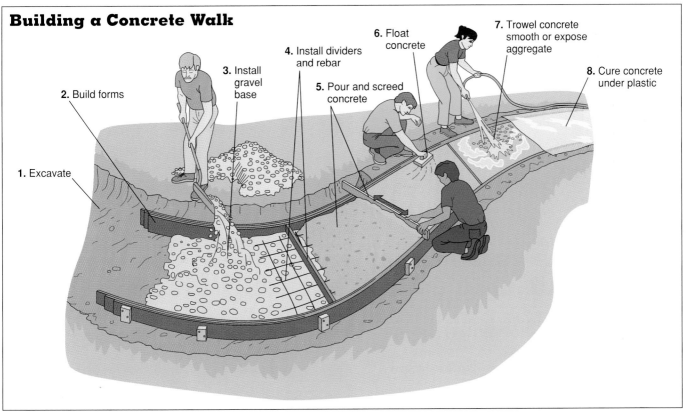

3. Install gravel base

4. Install dividers and rebar

6. Float concrete

7. Trowel concrete smooth or expose aggregate

8. Cure concrete under plastic

2. Build forms

5. Pour and screed concrete

1. Excavate

Building a Brick-in-Mortar Walk

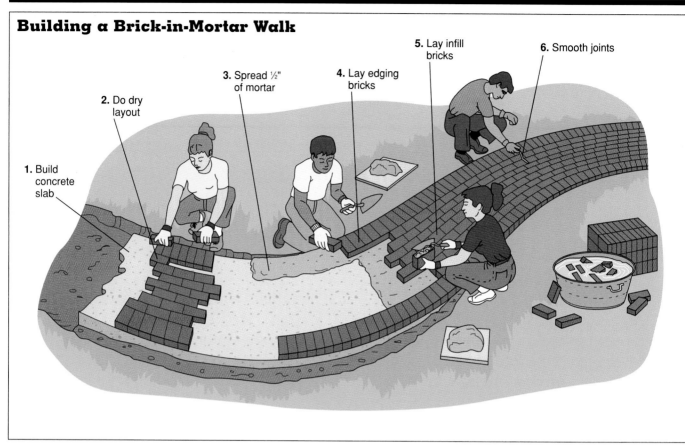

5. Lay infill bricks

6. Smooth joints

3. Spread ½" of mortar

4. Lay edging bricks

2. Do dry layout

1. Build concrete slab

Edgings for Walks

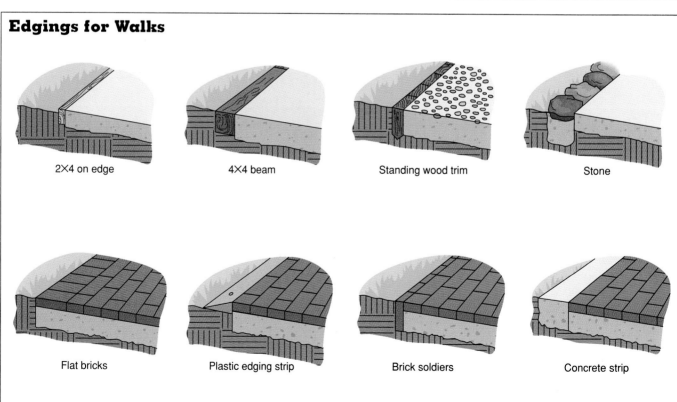

2×4 on edge

4×4 beam

Standing wood trim

Stone

Flat bricks

Plastic edging strip

Brick soldiers

Concrete strip

Raised edgings for either walks or gardens often present a difficulty, however. They frustrate your efforts with a lawn mower because the cutting blade can't get close enough to the grass. This usually means going back over the area with a weed trimmer or pair of clippers. A solution to this problem is to lay a treated 4×4 up against the edging flush with the ground, so the lawn mower wheel can run along it (you may need to experiment to see what height will work with your lawn mower). Make sure to use weed control fabric under both the 4×4 and the edging material so no weeds grow in the cracks.

Steps

The style of steps built into the ground should be clearly defined and dramatic. The design should invite your guests to stroll through the garden, and should lead the eye smoothly between the separate but related levels of the site.

A special consideration in the design of steps is safety. They should have a nonskid surface so they aren't slippery when wet. Steps should be uniform in height and width. A handrail is required for any stairway with more than a certain number of steps (usually two). The height of a handrail should be 30 to 34 inches above the tread nosings. The ends of the railings should extend slightly beyond the bottom and top steps and should terminate in a post or wall in such a way that a person's sleeve cannot hook onto a protruding end. The rail itself must be fully grippable.

All hardware should be galvanized to retard rust.

Take special care in calculating riser and tread dimensions used in building the steps. Although garden steps may offer a bit more leeway than a flight of stairs, outdoor steps should meet the same requirements that stairs do. The tread area must be wide and stable underfoot, and the risers should not be so high that moving up and down is an effort. Risers for garden steps should not be less than 4½ inches and not more than 7 inches; around 6 inches is preferred. As with stairs, all risers except the first must be of equal height to prevent trip-

Calculating Garden Steps

In planning the number of steps, you must figure the angle of the slope. Start by driving a stake where the top step will be. Directly in line with that stake, at the bottom of the slope, drive a stake that is tall enough to be at least level with the top of the slope. Stretch a length of string or a straight 2×4 from the top of the top stake directly over the bottom stake. Use a level to keep the string or board level. Measure the vertical distance from the bottom of the slope up to the string or board, and measure the horizontal length of the level piece. That gives you the total rise and run of the stairs (see illustration below). If each riser will be 7 inches high, divide the total rise by 7 to see how many risers will be required. Round the answer down to the nearest whole number. Next, divide that whole number of risers back into the total rise to determine the exact height of each riser. Then adjust the total run so that the treads are the proper width for the exact height of the risers.

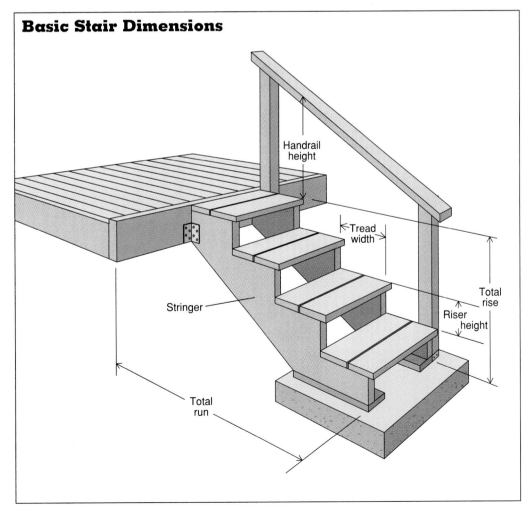

Basic Stair Dimensions

Handrail height

Tread width

Stringer

Total rise

Riser height

Total run

ping; the first riser may be shorter than the others. All treads must be of equal width (measured front to back). Keep this rule in mind: the lower the riser, the wider the tread. This makes for both comfortable walking and eye appeal. Wide treads also make inviting places for seating or for plant containers.

The side-to-side dimension of your steps will depend on your site and design, but landscape designers generally make them about 4 feet across. In garden paths, where steps may be far apart, space steps evenly so people will not have to change stride repeatedly.

Step material is often chosen to complement materials used elsewhere in the landscape. The possibilities include stone, concrete, brick, and railroad ties. If you're buying stone at a masonry yard, ask to see material that can be used for step treads. You may be able to have the stone cut and faced at the yard, though do so only if you're confident of your measurements.

Driveways

A well-designed driveway can make access to your home easy and pleasant. A wide driveway with a parking bay allows more than one car to use it. If you have enough space, you may design a curve wide enough for two cars. Narrow straight driveways have little eye appeal and are inconvenient if regularly used by more than one car.

If you have a narrow driveway but your budget doesn't permit a new one, consider adding a parking bay off to the side. If possible, match the surface material of the existing drive; if not, try slightly colored gravel for the additional parking spot. The object is to avoid a glaring difference in materials.

Design Basics

The width of a single driveway should be 11 to 12 feet; this allows passengers to exit a car without having to step off the driveway. If you have a narrow driveway, you might build a walkway along each side, edging the walkways with plants. Bricks, paving blocks, or cut flat stone would work well since they provide a flat, even footing. Gravel and other loose material may cause safety and snow-removal problems.

A driveway should slope no more than 2 percent within the first 20 feet of the garage door, and no more than 4 to 10 percent thereafter until it joins the public street or road, where it should be as level as possible. Changes in slope must be gradual to prevent cars from scraping bottom.

Another factor to consider is drainage. A driveway should slope away from the house, so water will not run into the garage. Or you can make a slight drainage depression between the garage slab and driveway grade; the depression should be lower than both. Lead the water away to a dry well on the side.

When you are evaluating your driveway, consider effective screening to separate the car area from a private retreat. You can add a latticework screen, wall, or fence. Shrubs and flower beds, or vines on a fence, take the harshness out of all that concrete, asphalt, stone. However, as you develop a screening plan, don't overlook security. You want a clear line of sight from the closest door of your house to the place where you leave the car. This is one area you don't want to have secluded or screened. In addition, a driveway should be lighted. Sensor floodlights that come on when a car or pedestrian comes up the drive may be the most effective. Low-voltage lighting can be used to highlight walks and even the driveway itself.

Garden steps that, compared to interior stairs, have lower risers and correspondingly deeper treads tend to invite a leisurely stroll among the flowers.

Recommended Driveway Dimensions

Door
8' single
16' double

13'

18' parking length

10' radius

11'

Turning area

A

B

8'   10'

Additional length for full turnaround (driveway B)

11' single drive
20' double drive

Materials

Driveways can be made of a variety of materials. Two of the most common are concrete and asphalt. In suburban or rural areas, you'll also find crushed stone and gravel. Another common material is interlocking block, brick, or granite cobblestone (although these can be expensive). In rural areas a driveway may be just a dirt road, but this will present problems if there are prolonged heavy rains.

When shopping for materials like paving blocks or bricks, make sure they are rated for driveway use. If they aren't, you could end up with cracked blocks the first time a heavy truck pulls in to deliver a new refrigerator or pick up garbage.

Construction

Essentially, driveway construction is similar to walk construction but on a larger scale. The site must be excavated, a compacted base must be laid, and the paving material installed. Such work requires heavy-duty equipment, such as a bulldozer and dump truck for soil removal, and plenty of hard labor. Most do-it-yourselfers should leave driveway construction to professionals. Confine your efforts to the expansion or repair of an existing gravel drive—and undertake that job only if you are ambitious and hale. If your yen for moving earth is undeniable, consider renting a small scoop loader and constructing a berm from the soil removed from the driveway site.

Driveways and parking spaces don't have to be expressionless expanses of concrete. Many other landscape-construction materials, such as this paving brick, can be used instead.

THE PRIVATE RETREAT

The core of your backyard retreat is the living space: space where you can sit and relax, entertain friends, or cook up a barbecue—in comfort and privacy. The easiest way to create such a space is to construct a deck or patio. Or even both!

This chapter presents design guidelines and examples of decks and patios for outdoor living. It covers construction basics for both projects and shows you how to solve such problems as building on a slope, providing drainage for a patio, and weatherproofing. You will also find guidelines for planning and building overheads and for planning and selecting a spa or sauna to complete your backyard retreat.

This patio invites outdoor living. Centered on the pool, it has a comfortable seating area, tables for entertaining, and lights for night use.

DECKS

Adding a deck is one of the easiest and fastest ways to create outdoor living space. You can build a deck almost anywhere, and once you get beyond the framing, it's as easy as cutting and fastening boards.

Designing a Deck

Deck design begins with questions. How do you want to use the deck? Will it be an extension of your indoor living space? Will you want separate areas for children and adults? Do you do a lot of entertaining? Do you prefer intimacy and privacy? Answer those questions, and all the others—size, location, type, and shape—generally fall into place.

Most deck construction requires a building permit, which means drawing up plans, making copies, and submitting them to the building inspection office. The plans may be as simple as drawings showing lumber dimensions, footing depths, and framing design. If you are tempted not to get a permit in order to

Two types of wood commonly used for building decks are pressure-treated pine (top) and redwood (bottom).

avoid an increase in property taxes, consider the problems and delays that you may face later—when selling your home—and the peace of mind that comes from knowing your deck was built properly.

Size and Proportions

A deck should be about the same size as the indoor room intended for the same purpose. A deck for intimate dining would be dining room size; a deck for cooking and entertaining should be the size of a kitchen and a family room combined. Bigger decks are not necessarily better. A big attached deck, if it's out of proportion to the house, distorts the whole plan. A large deck may also lack the sense of intimacy.

Only you can determine the size of the deck that will suit your "comfort level." However, you may want to follow what is called the golden mean in regard to the size of a deck. Roughly translated, it prescribes 5 feet of deck for every 7 feet of house, matching width to width and depth to depth. This 5:7 ratio creates a natural balance in the proportion of deck to house. (There isn't any proportional standard that uses the size of a yard to help determine the size of a deck.) Thus, a house about 28 feet wide should have a deck roughly 20 feet wide.

Another reason why you shouldn't make your deck too large is a practical one: the bigger the deck, the more expensive it will be and the more maintenance it will require.

Tip: Keep in mind that lumber is generally sold in 2-foot increments. Using dimensions divisible by an even number will help reduce wasted lumber and construction costs. For solid decking, use 2×4, 2×6, or ¾-inch decking lumber over joists spaced 16 or 24 inches apart on center. (Of course, the size of the deck will also be affected by the span and spacing requirements for the posts, beams, and joists.)

When planning your deck, consider making perimeter posts tall enough to protrude through the deck and serve as railing posts.

Wheelchair Access

When planning any deck or backyard landscape, consider that mobility is not necessarily a permanent condition. At some time or another we may all experience some form of mobility impairment due to accident, aging, disease, work injury, or even pregnancy. As you design your landscape, try to avoid impediments to mobility and provide wheelchair access where feasible.

By usually accepted standards, a properly constructed wheelchair ramp has a rise of 1 inch for every 12 inches of horizontal run, or a ratio of 1:12. No one ramp run should be longer than 30 feet. If a turn must be made, there must be a level platform at the end of each run. The platform should be about 5 feet wide. For example, a deck surface 4 feet off the ground requires a 48-foot-long ramp. At a minimum, this means two runs, each 24 feet in length, with one 5-foot platform at the turn. Ramps should be at least 3 feet wide. A handrail 32 inches high, and extending 1 foot beyond the top and bottom of the ramp, must be installed. For additional information on disabled access, contact the county department of human services or a similar agency that deals with access issues; consult local codes to determine if different requirements apply in your area.

Building a ramp is like building a minideck. Wood should be pressure-treated, posts need to be set in concrete, and the stringers must be sturdy enough not to sag. Bolt all stringers to posts and use posts for railing supports.

The elements of this deck—ramp, railings, and bench—blend together well, making it attractive as well as comfortable and accessible.

Layout for a Deck

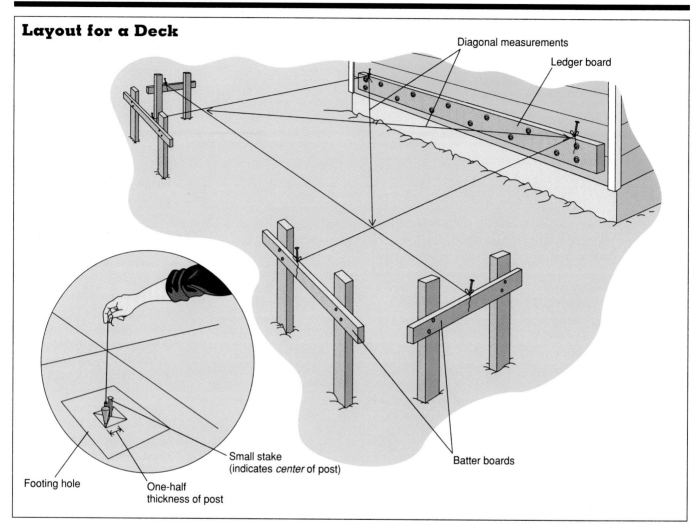

Diagonal measurements

Ledger board

Batter boards

Small stake (indicates *center* of post)

Footing hole

One-half thickness of post

Light and Shade

When you are considering deck design, keep in mind where the sun will shine and how you want to light the deck at night.

The hot summer sun beating down on a deck may make the space unusable during certain parts of the day. Without any shade, such a deck will seem like a waste. One solution to this problem is building an overhead (see page 72). Or, if you can take a long-term view, plant a shade tree.

Since nighttime lighting will be necessary at some point, you should plan for it at this stage. On the deck you'll probably want an outlet with a ground fault circuit interrupter (GFCI), low-voltage lighting around the perimeter and steps, and a method of overall deck and yard illumination (see page 29).

Construction

Your working drawings and detailed drawings are your guides for post locations, footing depths, lumber dimensions, framing connections, and other details. First, clear

off the site—particularly wood debris and vegetation—and grade it so water will drain away from the house. To discourage weeds and burrowing animals, lay weed control fabric over the site and cover it with gravel (this covering will interfere slightly with excavation and concrete work as you build the footings, but now is the easiest time to do it).

If the deck will be attached to the house, install the ledger board first—you will use it as a reference for layout. To prevent moisture from getting trapped behind the ledger,

tuck metal flashing under the siding boards and over the ledger top, or install plastic or aluminum spacers between the ledger and siding.

Build batter boards and lay out the footing locations with string lines.

Footings and Piers

Although some decks are supported by pressure-treated posts buried directly in the ground and backfilled with gravel, most deck posts have concrete piers and footings. The piers are either precast

Deck Footings

Precast Pier

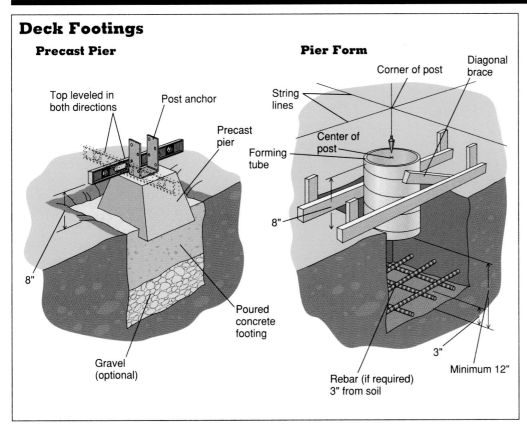

Top leveled in both directions

Post anchor

Precast pier

8"

Gravel (optional)

Poured concrete footing

Pier Form

String lines

Corner of post

Diagonal brace

Center of post

Forming tube

8"

3"

Minimum 12"

Rebar (if required) 3" from soil

Deck Framing

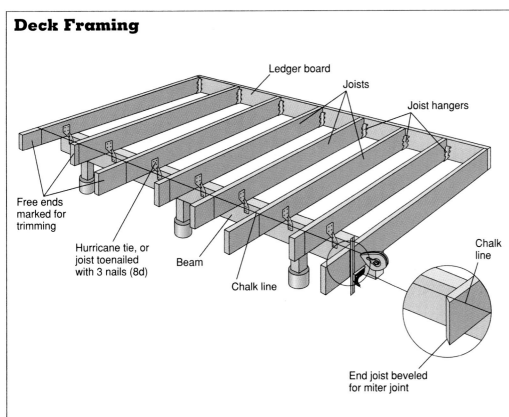

Ledger board

Joists

Joist hangers

Free ends marked for trimming

Hurricane tie, or joist toenailed with 3 nails (8d)

Beam

Chalk line

Chalk line

End joist beveled for miter joint

blocks set into the footing concrete or the top portion of the footings themselves. If the piers are cast with the footings, they extend at least 8 inches above grade and are shaped by cardboard forming tubes or other site-built forms. This type of pier, and the better types of precast piers, have a bracket embedded in them for anchoring the post. The footings are simply concrete poured into holes dug to just below the frost line. Or, where climates are mild, the holes are dug to a minimum depth of 12 inches. If you plan to pour the footings yourself, see pages 24 to 27 for general information about estimating, mixing, working with, and curing concrete. Consult the local building department to learn the required depth and width. Local law may require the building inspector to check the footing depth and reinforcing steel, so call for an inspection before you pour concrete.

If using precast pier blocks, soak them in water for several minutes before setting them into wet concrete. Level the top of the concrete with a wood float or scrap of 2×4 and let the concrete stiffen slightly. If using a metal post bracket, set it into the wet concrete; then embed the precast pier block. Use a torpedo level to align it horizontally and vertically.

Building the Deck

After the concrete has cured for a day or two, install the posts. Cut them longer than needed, then trim them after erecting them. Unless a post will extend all the way to the railing, mark it for cutting by

Nailing and Trimming Decking

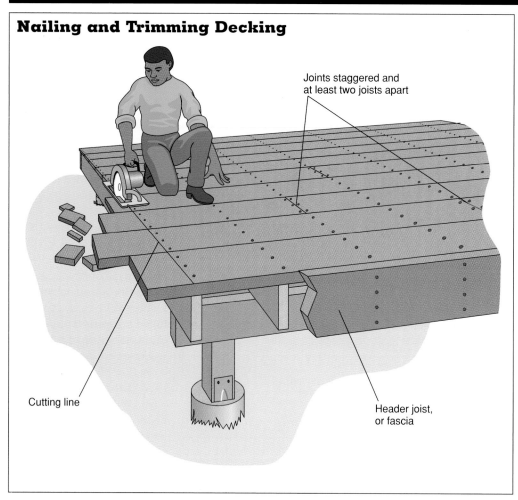

Joints staggered and at least two joints apart

Cutting line

Header joint, or fascia

Typical Stair Dimensions

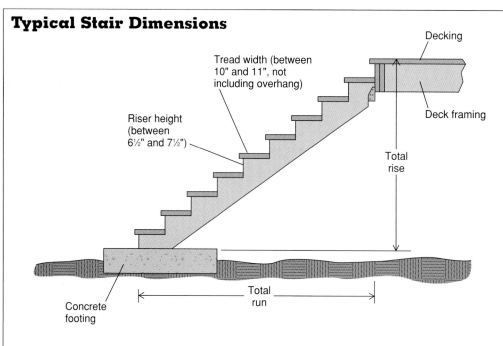

Tread width (between 10" and 11", not including overhang)

Riser height (between 6½" and 7½")

Decking

Deck framing

Total rise

Total run

Concrete footing

extending a level line from the top of the ledger board to the post. Then measure down from that line a distance equal to the depth of both the joist and the beam.

Attach beams to the tops of the posts with metal connectors. Mark the joist layout on the ledger and the beam. Then install each joist by attaching one end to the ledger board with a joist hanger and toenailing the other end to the beam. For a stronger connection, reinforce the toenailing with hurricane ties. The free end of the joist can extend beyond the beam (cantilever), but no more than half the distance between the ledger and the beam. Nail a header joist across the free ends of the joists, then install blocking between joists at the beam.

Lay the deck boards out on the joists, placing the best pieces against the house, at the edge of the deck, and at stairs or other access points. Attach the boards with galvanized deck screws or twist nails, with a slight gap between boards. Use a spacer to ensure that the width of the gaps is uniform. From time to time, take measurements out from the house to each edge to keep the boards even. After the decking is installed, trim off the ends of the boards.

Stairs

Stair building is a specialized process in which the measurements are everything. To build stairs you need two 2×12 boards for stringers and a carpenter's framing square; for stairs 4 feet or wider, use a third stringer. Deck stairs should have a ratio of 6 inches

Laying Out a Stair Stringer

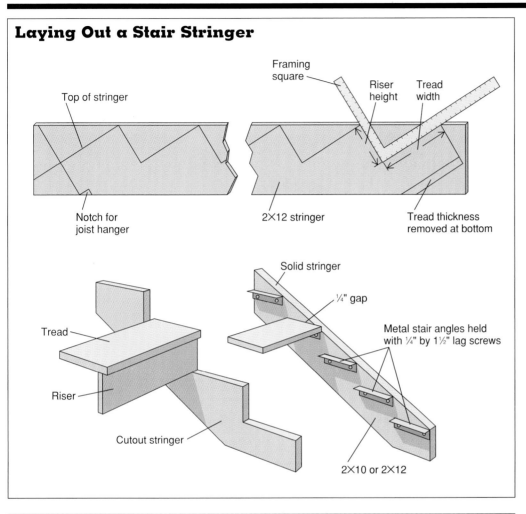

Top of stringer

Notch for joist hanger

Framing square

Riser height

Tread width

2×12 stringer

Tread thickness removed at bottom

Solid stringer

Tread

Riser

Cutout stringer

¼" gap

Metal stair angles held with ¼" by 1½" lag screws

2×10 or 2×12

Simple can be sophisticated: intimate size, light color, low benches, and easy access to the yard are some of the elements that give this deck its appeal.

of rise for 12 inches of tread (household stairs are usually a ratio of 7:11).

Measure the distance from the deck to the landing. Then, using the riser height you prefer, apply the method explained on page 53 to estimate how many steps are needed. Mark the stringer with the framing square. In this case the framing square is placed with one leg intersecting the edge of the board at 12 inches (for the tread) and the other leg intersecting it at 6 inches (for the riser). The top step should be the exact riser height below the decking, or flush with it. The riser distance between the last step and the landing pad can be a little less than the others, if that helps make the other steps the same height.

Mark the first stringer, cut it with a power saw, and check your work by putting it in place. If it fits, use it as a pattern for cutting the second stringer. After cutting out the stringers, attach the tops to the deck with bolts or joist hangers. The bottoms should rest on a brick or concrete pad—never on bare ground where they would decay. Finally, cut the treads to length and screw or nail them to the stringers.

Railings

Check with the local building department for code requirements. A railing is required around a deck if it is a certain height off the ground, usually 18 inches. There are also code requirements for the height of the railing (typically 36 inches) and for the space between the railing members (typically 4 inches). When there are more

Sample Railing Configurations

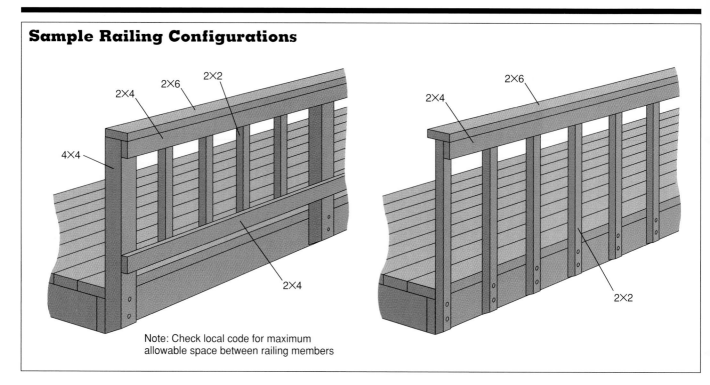

Note: Check local code for maximum allowable space between railing members

than a certain number of steps in a flight of stairs—usually two or three—a railing is usually mandatory.

Railing design can be elaborate or simple. A railing can help define the deck as formal and traditional, or it can give it a more contemporary look. You can integrate railing posts with seating by adding benches; slope the back for comfort.

Deck Finishes

After the deck is completed and the wood has seasoned a few weeks, apply a protective finish, even if you've used redwood, cedar, cypress, or pressure-treated lumber. See page 29 for more finishing tips.

Many homeowners choose to paint their decks. Realize that, before being painted, a deck should be protected with a quality sealer. Sealers are water repellents that protect wood from moisture but leave it looking natural because they

are clear. Some include preservatives. After the sealer has dried, apply a quality paint. (Work on cool, windless days so the paint won't dry too quickly.) Paints designed for marine use are an excellent (although expensive) choice. The drawback to paint is that you may have to repaint the deck every few years. If you want to avoid this kind of maintenance, don't paint the deck at all—just coat it with the sealer. Or stain the deck floor, and seal and paint just the vertical surfaces, such as railings.

Stains seal wood and come in a variety of tints or colors. They are easier to apply than paint. Ask for a stain that is nonchalking so it won't rub off on clothes. Before staining, the deck should have stood in hot dry weather for at least a month so the wood will absorb the stain like a sponge. For best results, mix the stain with an equal amount of sealer.

Your deck does not have to put you on stage. The enclosure around this deck gives it privacy and wind protection, without sacrificing views and openness.

Like decks, patios provide outdoor living space. A patio is generally a fixed masonry platform set in sand, mortar, or concrete. It can be freestanding, set against a house, or tiered on a slope and connected by steps.

Designing a Patio

Start by listing all the activities for which you and your family will use the patio. Consider what kind of space and facilities each person needs. You'll see that some activities can share the same space but others have opposing requirements—some may need sunshine, others shade; some may need a large, open area, others an intimate, sheltered space. You may have to give up some uses—or plan more than one patio. Patterns will emerge that will help you plan. In addition, consider location, size, and materials.

Location and Size

In choosing a location, consider privacy and access to the house and backyard. Do you want the patio to be secluded and private? Do you want it to be readily accessed, maybe part of the natural traffic path?

Make use of existing desirable features. You can build a patio around a tree, for instance. If you do, remember that the tree needs water to survive. A wide tree well and a sand base for the patio will let water and air into the soil, but a concrete or mortar patio may end up killing the tree.

On the other hand, avoid damp locations, which can cause problems with mildew, slippery pavement, and insects such as mosquitoes.

Plan the size in proportion to the house. You may want to use the 5:7 ratio (see page 59).

However, it is not a hard and fast rule. Keep in mind that you can use walls, planters, flower beds, and other dividers to modify the perceived shape. A long, winding walkway can make a small patio seem larger. If the patio is enclosed, say with hedges, a small trellis at the entrance can make it seem larger. An overhead placed at the far end of a large patio can make it feel smaller and cozier. Or, instead of a large patio, make two small patios, connected by a walk. Whatever you decide, the size should be able to accommodate the activities planned for the patio.

Suggestion: To help visualize size, set out the patio furniture, grill, and other furnishings and have family and friends comfortably occupy the area in which you want to make the patio. When you think you have settled on a size and shape, mark the boundary with a garden hose.

Materials

You have a wide choice of materials, including concrete, brick, tile, flagstone, and pavers. The color and style of what you choose should blend with your home and property. Avoid any material that will become slippery when wet. Be aware that some stone absorbs the sun's rays and may become too hot to walk on in bare feet. Also consider ease of installation. Setting bricks or pavers on a sand base is fairly easy to do. Pouring a concrete slab with a smooth finish is much harder. However, many

Convenient access to the house, pleasant views, a striking fountain, a sense of enclosure—this patio has it all.

homeowners would be able to pour a concrete slab as a base for setting flagstones, bricks, or other paving in mortar, although the process is time-consuming and tedious.

Tip: In many areas, constructing a patio does not require a building permit. But adding a patio could increase your property taxes, depending on whether it is set on a concrete base or in sand. You may want to ask the local assessor.

Construction

Constructing a patio is similar to building a walk (see pages 49 to 53), except on a larger scale. Techniques vary depending on whether you are laying the paving materials on a sand base or a concrete slab. Whichever type you build, first clear the site. The next step is to lay out the patio perimeter and excavate for the base.

Layout and Excavation

Use batter boards and string lines to lay out the boundaries. All the batter boards should be level to establish a stable reference for determining the depth and slope of the excavation. Lay out curves and rounded edges by marking their position with a series of stakes or by pouring gypsum, chalk, or flour in a line on the ground. For free-form curves, shape a garden hose into the outline you want and use it as a guide for setting the stakes or pouring the chalk. For a precisely measured curve, drive a stake at the center point of the curve

Top: Laying bricks on a sand base makes it easy to build a large and beautiful patio, such as this one.
Center: A flagstone patio with mortared joints requires a concrete slab as the base, to keep the stones stable.
Bottom: Concrete doesn't have to be drab. The exposed aggregate surface, divider boards, and curved edges of this patio dress it up nicely.

Excavating for a Patio

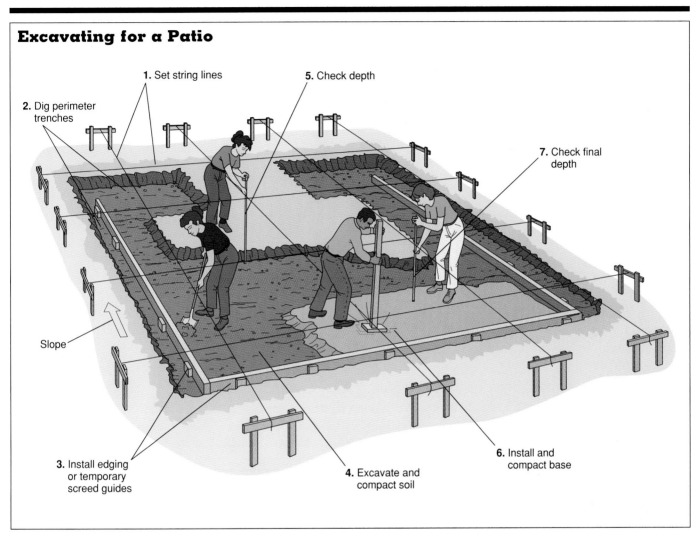

1. Set string lines

5. Check depth

2. Dig perimeter trenches

7. Check final depth

Slope

3. Install edging or temporary screed guides

4. Excavate and compact soil

6. Install and compact base

and tie a string to it. Then measure a distance along the string that is equal to the radius of the curve, tie a nail to the string at that point, pull the string taut, and scratch an arc on the ground with the nail. Follow up with chalk.

In excavating, the goal is a smooth soil base at the right depth, sloped for drainage. This is strictly shovel, wheelbarrow, and muscle work. Do the heavy work in the mornings or evenings, when the air is cooler, and drink plenty of liquids to replace water lost by sweat and evaporation. Avoid overdigging, so you won't

have to backfill low spots. To gauge depth, stretch new string lines at 5-foot intervals, so they crisscross the patio area in a grid pattern. Measure down from these lines to guide your digging. Adjust your measurements for the desired slope of the patio.

Tip: The soil you remove may be used for filling raised planter beds. To salvage the soil from the grass, use a turf remover or vigorously shake the soil loose. Throw the grass onto the compost pile.

Building a Concrete Patio

Around the perimeter of the proposed patio, dig a shallow trench for 2×4 forms. Stake the forms so the top edges will be at the height of the finished slab. If the patio is near the house, make sure the forms have a slight pitch away from the house. Then excavate the soil inside the forms to a depth of 8 inches below the slab surface. Patios where winters are severe require deeper footings around the perimeter, so you will have to dig a trench for them (check locally accepted practice for footing dimen-

sions). Fill the excavation (but not footing trenches) to the bottom of the form boards with sand or gravel. Compact it with a short length of 4×4, the flat side of a concrete block, or a plate vibrator that you can rent.

Before pouring the concrete, place reinforcing mesh or a grid of No. 3 rebar at 12-inch intervals inside the forms. Raise it off the base with 2-inch dobies (concrete blocks) or use a garden rake to pull it up after the concrete is placed. Pour the concrete, strike it off, and float it using a darby (see pages 25 to 27).

Forms Ready for Concrete

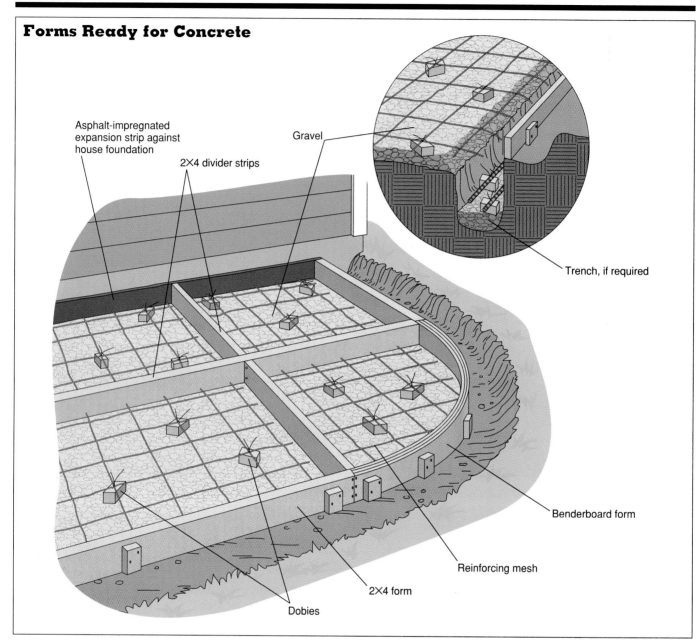

Asphalt-impregnated expansion strip against house foundation

2×4 divider strips

Gravel

Trench, if required

Benderboard form

Reinforcing mesh

2×4 form

Dobies

If the concrete is the finished surface, you can give it a specialized finish by using a variety of finishing tools; you can even add coloring. Broom finishes and aggregate finishes you may be able to do yourself, but leave a smooth finish to an experienced contractor; ask your masonry supplier for recommendations. Be sure to look at the contractor's work on other people's patios. See-

ing a finish technique on a large scale is different from seeing only a small sample or a photograph.

Adding a Stone or Brick Surface

Bricks or stones laid in mortar require a concrete base. Build the base as you would a concrete patio and finish the surface with a wood float; a smooth finish is not necessary.

When the concrete is fully cured (in about 7 days), you are ready to use it as a base for brick, flagstone, tile, or whatever material you've chosen.

To install the paving, first set screed guides around the slab. They should protrude about ½ inch above the slab for bricks, 1 inch for stone. Working in small areas, spread mortar over the slab. (For tips on using mortar, see the chart

and text on page 21.) If using bricks, soak them in water ahead of time; apply mortar to one side and one end of each brick as you lay it into place. Stretch mason's twine along each course or row of bricks that you lay, to keep them aligned. Strike off excess mortar, keeping the bricks clean as you work. After laying a few courses, or rows, go back over the fresh mortar joints with a

Finishing Concrete

Broom

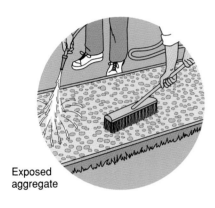

Exposed
aggregate

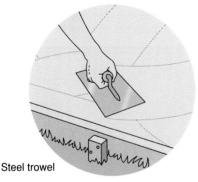

Steel trowel

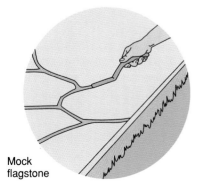

Mock
flagstone

jointing tool, to smooth and shape them. Again, clean off all excess mortar. After completing the installation, spray the joints with a fine mist periodically over two days. This will help the mortar cure to maximum strength.

Space stones ½ inch apart, and give them a rap to set them. Lay a level over several stones to check alignment. Let the paving set overnight, then fill the joints with mortar, using a grout bag and finishing with a jointing tool. Kneel on a sheet of plywood to distribute your weight. As you set the paving and mortar the joints, clean off excess mortar with a trowel, then a damp rag. If stains remain, wait 24 hours and clean the surface with a mixture of 1 part muriatic acid added to 10 parts water, following instructions on the acid container. Wear eye protection and rubber gloves. Scrub the surface with a heavy-duty sponge or burlap sack.

Suggestion: If you already have a concrete patio and don't like it, consider using it as a base for a brick or stone patio. You may need to install an edging of soldier (upright) bricks or wood to conceal the edges of the paving.

Building a Brick-in-Sand Patio

Excavate the area to be paved to a depth of 4 to 6 inches (2 to 4 inches below the depth of the brick). As edging, install redwood, cedar, or pressure-treated 2×4s, 4×4s, or 6×6s and toenail them together with galvanized spikes. Or embed soldier bricks in the dirt or in

concrete, or form and pour a concrete curb. Place 4 to 6 inches of gravel within the enclosed area. Cover the gravel with 2 inches of sand to bring the base within 2 inches of the finished surface. Moisten the sand and screed it level by dragging a 2×4 across the surface. To ensure proper depth, notch 2¼ inches (the thickness of one brick) from the bottom side of each end of the 2×4 so the ends will fit over the edges and the bottom edge of the board will level the sand exactly 2¼ inches below the finished brick surface. After leveling the sand, dampen and compact it. You can tamp it with a homemade ram consisting of a 12-inch square of plywood nailed to the end of a stout timber, but it is easier and more effective to rent a plate vibrator. Lay a sheet of weed-blocking fabric on top of the sand. Then use the 2×4 screed to check for level, adding more sand as necessary.

After leveling and compacting any added sand, lay the bricks in the pattern of your choice. Fit them tightly against each other, cutting to fit where necessary. Tap each brick with a rubber mallet as you set it, and check your work periodically with a straight board. Even out the high spots and low spots by removing or building up sand. After laying the bricks, spread fine sand over the installation and sweep it into the cracks between the bricks. Finally, run the plate vibrator over the bricks a few times to lock them in place, using sheets of plywood to protect the brick surface. (For more installation tips, see pages 20 to 22.)

Laying Flagstone Over a Concrete Base

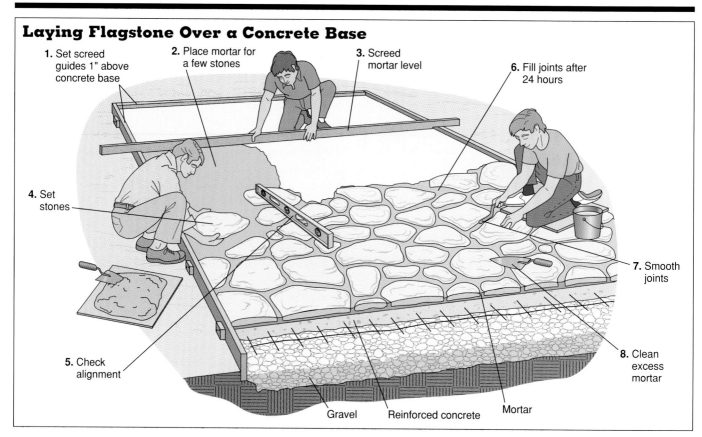

1. Set screed guides 1" above concrete base

2. Place mortar for a few stones

3. Screed mortar level

6. Fill joints after 24 hours

4. Set stones

5. Check alignment

7. Smooth joints

8. Clean excess mortar

Gravel   Reinforced concrete   Mortar

Laying Bricks on Sand

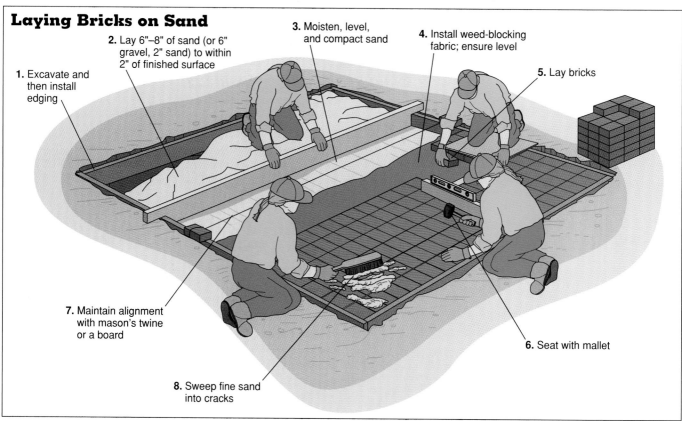

1. Excavate and then install edging

2. Lay 6"–8" of sand (or 6" gravel, 2" sand) to within 2" of finished surface

3. Moisten, level, and compact sand

4. Install weed-blocking fabric; ensure level

5. Lay bricks

7. Maintain alignment with mason's twine or a board

6. Seat with mallet

8. Sweep fine sand into cracks

Using Dry Mortar to Build a Patio

Building a patio with dry mortar between the bricks is similar to building a brick-in-sand patio, but you leave a ¼-inch gap between bricks, then fill the gaps with a mixture of 1 part portland cement to 3 parts dry sand. Use a broom to sweep the mixture into the joints. Then, using a fine spray, soak the entire area. Repeat spraying after 15 minutes. After the bricks dry, add another layer of mix to fill in any settled areas. Soak new mix with spray. Clean all excess mix from the brick surface.

Drainage

Unless you want an ice skating rink in winter or a frog pond in summer, plan for some drainage. If the patio is near the house, give it a slight pitch when you're setting up the concrete forms or screeding the sand, so water runs onto the yard, not into the basement. If you are unable to establish a slope, try to keep the surface flush with the grade, but not below it. You may want to lay drainpipe along the perimeter, in a bed of gravel, to direct runoff into a dry well. Another option is to set a recessed drain grate into the floor of the patio and connect it to a dry well. (The illustration on page 16 shows a cross section of a dry well.)

Waterproofing

Once you've finished the patio, take steps to waterproof it. Water will seep into joints and freeze, which will cause cracks that will become bigger

and eventually result in broken brick or stone. A clear sealer will help prevent this. Sealer will also help prevent moss on the patio surface. Apply the sealer annually. If you have a stained or weathered patio, scrub it first with a solution of 5 percent muriatic acid (1 part acid to 20 parts water). Rinse well, wait a week, then apply sealer.

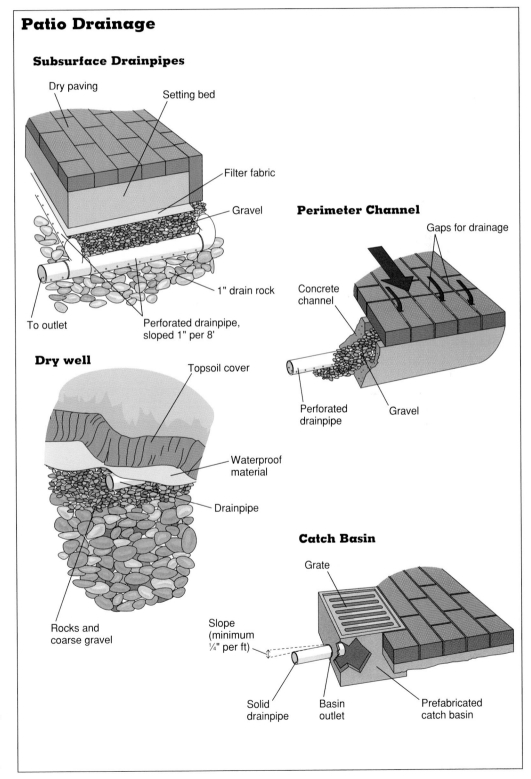

Patio Drainage

Subsurface Drainpipes

Dry paving
Setting bed
Filter fabric
Gravel
1" drain rock
To outlet
Perforated drainpipe, sloped 1" per 8'

Perimeter Channel

Gaps for drainage
Concrete channel
Perforated drainpipe
Gravel

Dry well

Topsoil cover
Waterproof material
Drainpipe
Rocks and coarse gravel

Catch Basin

Grate
Slope (minimum ¼" per ft)
Solid drainpipe
Basin outlet
Prefabricated catch basin

OVERHEADS

So you've built a deck or added a patio, but somehow it isn't perfect. It all looks too bare. The answer may be to add an overhead structure, which will not only enhance the landscape, but provide shade and privacy too.

Designing an Overhead

Whether an overhead is an arbor, trellis, or pergola, its basic structure consists of columns or posts; bracing; a framework of beams and rafters; and a covering of latticework, lath, or similar repetitive material. Variations on the theme are endless. The main supports can range from stout timbers to lacy fretwork, from classical columns to rustic pillars of stone. They can be spaced far apart to emphasize the horizontal framing members, or close together to create rhythm. The frame can be a simple grid or an intricate sculpture. The whole overhead can be painted, stained, or left natural. Add vines and it becomes a leafy canopy; without, a dramatic silhouette. The following considerations will help get you started in your planning.

• Purpose: Will the overhead be primarily for looks, or will it serve a practical purpose? The most common purpose is to add shade. If it is mainly decorative, then how will its design go with the house and deck or patio?

• Shade: If the overhead is to provide shade, study how the sun falls on the space you want shaded. The varying position of the sun from season to season and at different times of the day obviously affects patterns of sunlight and shade. Take account of this effect in planning the orientation and spacing of the framing members. For instance, to protect you from the late afternoon sun during the summer, you may have to extend the overhead beyond the patio or deck area. If this is the case, align at least one edge of the overhead with the corresponding edge of the

When designing an overhead structure you must take into account not only the maximum distance that each member can span, but also the need for strong connections and, in some areas, additional lateral bracing.

Typical Overhead Construction

Egg Crate Style

Attaching an Overhead to a House Wall

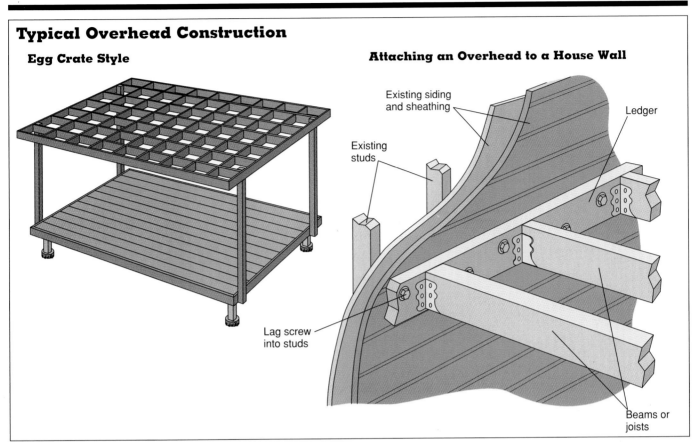

Existing siding and sheathing

Ledger

Existing studs

Lag screw into studs

Beams or joists

deck or patio, to maintain a harmonious relationship. If you can't solve the problem with an extension, consider planting a tree to do the job.

• Privacy: If you live in the city and have a tall building next to you, an overhead may be sufficient to give you privacy. In other settings, you may want to add lattice screening on the side. Small overheads can also screen utility areas from your deck, patio, house, or yard.

• Transitions: An overhead that covers a walkway can serve as a transition between the house and landscape elements. Landscape architects often use this technique when a house has a plain or flat exterior.

Construction

A simple overhead with wood posts and a grid of beams and rafters is a pleasant do-it-yourself project that will take just one or two weekends. The posts must be well anchored and braced against lateral movement. For the posts, use pressure-treated wood buried in the ground like fence posts, or attach posts to metal brackets set in concrete footings and add diagonal knee braces where the posts support the beams. If you want to put an overhead over your deck, plan ahead: When you build the deck, use tall perimeter posts that extend through the deck high enough to form the supports for the overhead. If retrofitting a deck, you will need to closely examine the

deck framing and consider the weight loads and placement of the posts. For best support, place the overhead posts directly over the deck posts.

Posts that support an overhead should be centered 6 to 12 feet apart, depending on the size of the beams. Headroom should be at least 7½ feet, so the posts should be no less than 7 feet high. Attach beams to the posts with T-straps or metal brackets and add knee braces to provide diagonal support, if needed.

Rafters can be any size, although the wider the spacing the larger they should be. Decorative cuts at the ends of the beams and the rafters are one of the keys to making an interesting overhead.

Add crosspieces to form a grid, either under or above the

rafters. You can also use 4×8 panels of wood or vinyl lattice.

If you are attaching the overhead to the house, fasten a ledger board to the wall close to the eave. It should be securely attached to the house and able to support several hundred pounds in the event you want to add a roof later. Use 5½-inch or larger lag screws fastened into the wall studs. The ledger board should be placed so that the overhead clears eaves and gutters.

After completing the overhead, give some thought to either painting or using stain or preservative. See page 29 for more details on finishes. Keep in mind that if you intend to have vines climb over the overhead, repainting will be difficult.

SPAS AND SAUNAS

The ultimate luxury in a private backyard retreat is a spa or sauna. Integrated with a deck or patio, either can be an attractive and useful feature of your yardscape—and offer some welcome self-indulgence as well.

Spas

Set in a pavilion or gazebo, a spa can be the focal point of a yard; screened with an overhead and trellis, it can blend into its surroundings. A portable spa can be made to look more permanent by setting it into a sheltered nook or building decking around it. If your climate is moderate all year, adding a spa is quite simple. If you live in an area where it gets very cold, then you need to make sure the unit is well insulated and be prepared to pay higher energy bills.

Because water, electrical wiring, and complicated plumbing are involved, a spa should be professionally installed. However, you can prepare the site and install whatever base is needed. A portable spa requires a concrete slab. A sunken spa requires a spa-shaped hole in the ground, deep enough to add sand for a base. Provision for a drain is also required.

Caution: Because of prolonged exposure to high temperatures, spas and saunas are not recommended for pregnant women and people with certain heart conditions. Consult with your doctor.

Choosing and Using a Spa

When shopping for a spa, look for a full-service dealer—a reputable firm that installs and services what it sells. You want to feel confident that the installation is safe and complies with all regulations. For the same reason, buy brand-name equipment that has been approved by appropriate standards organizations such as Underwriters' Laboratories. Check consumer magazines for spa ratings, and don't be reluctant to ask dealers for a "test drive." Yes, you can "wet-test" a spa—just ask the dealer for an appointment.

Spas come in a variety of sizes, both fixed and portable. The key elements, other than the tub, are the pump, heater, filter, and controls. These items can be sold individually or as a "skid pack," in which they are all mounted on a steel base. Skid packs are usually sold with portable spas.

Make sure the components you buy will function efficiently together. Sometimes components can be mismatched or undersized. You may decide after owning the spa for a while that you want a higher-capacity heater or air blower. Will the equipment configuration permit you to upgrade later?

After installing a spa, adopt a regular cleaning schedule. Maintenance is crucial because water temperatures between 100° and 104° F are a natural breeding ground for bacteria. Estimates report that five people in a 500- to 700-gallon spa create, in terms of bacterial density, the same environment as 250 people in a 25,000-gallon pool. Keeping the pool chemicals balanced is crucial to preventing algae and other growths.

Saunas

Saunas are popular in colder climates like the upper Midwest, New England, and any region where there is skiing—cross country or downhill. A sauna is essentially a heavily insulated box with an interior finished in cedar or redwood and a heater for making steam. Temperatures in a sauna range from 160° to 200° F. The heat is very dry; the process cleans the skin by causing you to sweat the dirt off. It also stimulates circulation and reduces muscular tension. A sauna must be installed in a small shed. It is best suited to a corner of the deck; a spot by the side of the

A deck must be reinforced to hold a spa: Filled with water and people, a spa can weigh as much as 240 pounds per square foot, whereas most decks are designed for only 50 pounds per square foot.

patio; or off by itself in a corner of the yard, secluded by tall shrubs. Your costs will depend on many factors: whether you have a shed available or need to build one, your choice of heat source, and size of the sauna. You can build a sauna yourself, buy a kit, or have one built for you. Heat can be provided by an electric, gas, or wood-burning stove.

Choosing and Using a Sauna

First decide on the size of the sauna (how many it will seat) and its location. Then decide on a design and what kind of shed will contain it. Depending on the heat source, you will need to run a 240-volt electrical circuit; install a gas line; or, if you want a wood-burning stove, ensure that you have a ready source of dense, seasoned wood that will produce adequate heat.

A prefabricated sauna can be assembled in several hours. Some manufacturers will take your specifications for a shed and send you a bundle of pre-cut materials customized to your dimensions. If you want to build one from scratch, you can buy the key materials (stove, rocks, hardware, and the like) from a sauna manufacturer or local distributor.

A sauna is a relatively low-maintenance item, as long as it is kept clean. However, before you use your sauna it must be cured, a fairly easy process that begins with a thorough

cleaning. This means removing all construction debris; vacuuming all sawdust from every surface; and using a damp cloth and a bucket of

warm water to wipe down the ceilings, lights, benches, floors, rocks—everything. Open the door and turn on the heater for 30 minutes so it can burn

off the protective coatings. Close the door, bring the room to 200° F, and leave it there for about six hours. Now you can enjoy your sauna.

Support equipment for a spa—pump, filter, and heater—should be located within 10 to 15 feet of the spa. The water heater inlet should be on the same level as the spa, and the pump and filter should be located below the spa water level.

GARDENING STRUCTURES

For most people, outdoor living includes gardening; they enjoy growing things. This chapter features projects that enhance gardens by making it easier to tend the plants or maintain the yard or by adding a decorative touch. The chapter starts with guidelines for planning and building sheds, so you can have convenient storage for your gardening and outdoor recreation equipment. Next are directions for building raised garden beds and planter boxes, plus ideas for building simple planters, trellises, and a compost bin to help you recycle yard waste. Perhaps you would like a pool or pond. Even a simple one that you build yourself can become a fascinating focal point for your garden, offering an opportunity to grow interesting aquatic plants and adding serenity and charm to the landscape.

Raised vegetable beds, such as those shown here and on page 86, enhance gardening in many ways. The contained soil can be worked easily and will drain better. The edging board provides a comfortable place to sit and to place tools. And the raised beds organize the garden into an attractive centerpiece of the yard.

SHEDS

No landscape is complete without a place for storing all the things needed to maintain it—hoses, rakes, mowers, and the like—as well as bicycles and outdoor recreation equipment. If your garage doesn't have abundant storage space—and few do—you can build a shed.

Shed-Planning Basics

Although an accessory building, a shed should not be a last-minute afterthought in a landscape design. Plan the location, style, interior layout, and structural details carefully, so your shed will be as satisfactory as possible. You might want to consider additional uses for your shed—it can also serve as a workshop or a playhouse, for instance. In terms of design, a shed can be anything from an architectural centerpiece to a secret hideout tucked behind a hedge or shrubs. Start planning by considering the best location and size for the shed.

Choosing Location and Size

Go back to the bubble plan you developed in the first chapter and see where a shed could be placed on your property. Here are some suggestions.

• Don't place it in the middle of the yard unless it is attractive enough to be the center of attention.

• Align the shed with other buildings or prominent features of the landscape.

• The style of the shed should match that of the house: If the house has siding, so should the shed. Paint the shed in the same color scheme as the house. If you don't want it too visible, consider screening it with a trellis or tall shrubs.

• The shed may need to be set back a certain number of feet from the property line, according to local zoning codes. Call the planning or building department to find out what the required setbacks are and what permits you might need.

• Check to see if a shed or greenhouse may result in higher property taxes. It may make a difference if the structure is classified as permanent or temporary—make sure you learn the local tax assessor's interpretation and build accordingly.

• Take into consideration the location of the sun, prevailing winds, shade trees, other buildings, major garden features, and accessibility.

• The size of the shed will evolve from decisions on how it will be used and what it will hold. To get an idea of how big a shed you'll need, lay out all the things that will take up floor space and measure them. Also consider lumber sizes.

You'll want at least one light and one outlet in the shed (see page 28). Make sure that the outlet is protected by a ground fault circuit interrupter (GFCI).

A lean-to shed tucked against the wall of the house provides convenient storage for garden equipment and other items used outdoors. When attaching a structure to the house, observe local building codes for earth-to-wood clearance, roof slope, and siding materials.

Choosing the Type of Shed

The type you choose will depend on intended uses, appearance requirements, budget, and who will build it. Consider, in addition, whether the shed should be a lean-to or freestanding structure, metal or wood, or built from a kit or from scratch.

Lean-to or Freestanding?

If you need just a small storage area, then consider a lean-to shed. A lean-to, which attaches to an existing building, is similar to a closet and is an easy-to-build project. It can be built anywhere there is a wall and a solid base, such as against the house on a deck or patio, or against the garage on a small concrete pad. Lean-tos generally range in size from 2×4 feet to 4×8 feet, with a height of 6 to 8 feet. There should be enough free space in front of the shed to allow you to maneuver around the doors when they are open—usually 5 to 6 feet.

More complex to build than a lean-to, a freestanding shed offers more flexibility in size, location, and appearance. A freestanding shed can be as small as 4×6 feet and as large as a small barn. Foundation possibilities include skids, posts set into the ground, concrete pier blocks, a slab, or a continuous-perimeter foundation of poured concrete or concrete blocks. In your area a freestanding shed may be considered an auxiliary structure subject to code restrictions in regard to height and other characteristics. To minimize

height, consider a slab foundation and walls slightly lower than standard 8-foot stud walls. To maximize interior headroom, the roof can be designed without cross-ties or low-sloping rafters. The classic Dutch barn roof, or gambrel roof, allows lower side walls while creating maximum headroom inside.

Metal or Wood?

Prefabricated metal sheds come in a variety of sizes and can be erected fairly quickly.

Their drawbacks are that they tend to need maintenance because they rust; they can't be as easily customized as wood; and they often lack windows or skylights and so are dark. If you're just parking a lawn mower and bikes, a metal shed may be fine.

Wood sheds also come in prefabricated kits, with unlimited design options. More substantial than metal, they are usually more complex to build but involve basic carpentry techniques that are familiar to most do-it-yourselfers.

Kit or Scratch-built?

You can buy a kit and build it yourself, have a kit installed on your property by an experienced crew, or build your own shed from scratch. Building it yourself from scratch does not necessarily mean saving a lot of money. You still have to buy materials, and wood can be expensive. You won't have the buying leverage of a kit-builder, and you may be tempted to buy higher grades of material than are available in kits. However, because you are buying readily available

Lean-to Shed Construction

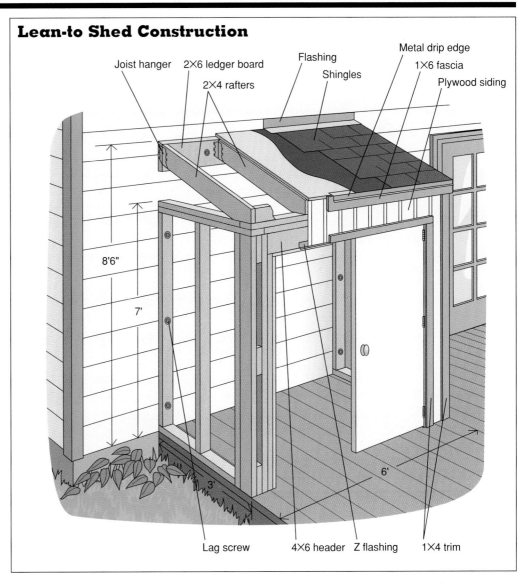

Joist hanger 2×6 ledger board Flashing Metal drip edge 1×6 fascia Plywood siding 2×4 rafters Shingles

8'6" 7' 3' 6'

Lag screw 4×6 header Z flashing 1×4 trim

materials, you will be able to shop for price, and you will save in labor costs.

Basing a cost estimate on square footage is not recommended. The best thing to do is to break out each component and cost it out. Develop a lumber list and ask several lumberyards to use it as the basis of a bid. Then compare the bids to the cost of a shed kit that includes delivery of materials—you supply the foundation and labor.

Kits range from inexpensive utilitarian designs to elaborate structures suitable for a home office or guest house. A kit may offer a more ornate design than you could create yourself or afford to have designed for you, but be aware that the kit won't be cheap either.

Some of the advantages to building a shed yourself are flexibility in design, greater control over the quality of materials, and the satisfaction of creating a complete building yourself. A shed is fairly easy to build; if you have basic carpentry skills, it can be a satisfying project that allows you to hone your skills before tackling something larger, like a deck. You can also take the time to add extra features and details that a kit may not include.

Greenhouses

A basic shed can be modified for many uses—for instance, with some interior finishing and fixtures, it can be a workshop, pool cabana, or children's playhouse. A greenhouse, however, is a very specialized structure that requires careful planning and construction; it needs to let in a lot of light and to retain heat during the colder months. The most important considerations are size, site, style, and covering. Here are some basic tips.

•Make the greenhouse larger than you anticipate using. Once you start greenhouse gardening, you will probably want to expand it.

•Determine what you will grow. Vegetables and flowers have different requirements from foliage houseplants.

•Estimate how much it will cost to heat and light the greenhouse to be sure you are willing to have the increases in your energy bill.

•Place the greenhouse where it will get at least six hours of direct sunlight each day. Orientation is important. An east-west greenhouse will take in about 25 percent more light than one situated north-south, since it has more surface at a right angle to the sun.

•Don't forget to factor in the snow load the roof may bear during the winter.

Building a Shed

Construction begins with a pencil, eraser, and paper (see pages 10 to 12). Plans should include dimensions and details of the foundation, framing, roofing, siding, trim, doors, windows, wiring, and interior layout. In detailed drawings show how framing connections will be made, such as how beams will connect to piers, how windows will be framed, and how wall plates will overlap. Making the drawings will help you visualize each step of construction. It will also help you make an accurate materials list, which is a prerequisite for an accurate price quotation. And the drawings will be useful in obtaining a permit, if required.

Greenhouse kits are easy to install. Most can be erected by two people in just a few hours. Some kits include a foundation, but most require that you build your own.

Here are some other tips for preparing for construction.

• Use pressure-treated lumber or plywood for all foundation beams, sills, floor joists, and flooring.

• Keep the foundation as simple as possible. On sites with adequate drainage, the easiest type consists of wood skids. Pier foundations require setting up batter boards and lines, and a poured concrete slab requires coordinating a concrete delivery and finishing the slab properly.

• Keep the construction site clean and well organized. Plan where you will store tools, dispose of scraps and debris, and pile the materials when they are delivered.

• Make sure that electrical tools and extension cords are plugged into outlets that are protected with GFCIs.

• Avoid the "I'll do it later" syndrome. For example, even if you aren't planning to wire the shed immediately, dig the trench and install the feeder or conduit cable now, rather than after the shed is built. You can terminate it in a junction box inside the shed.

Foundation

The types of foundations that most homeowners can build consist of skids, pier blocks, or a concrete slab. Whichever type you build, choose a site that is flat and has the necessary drainage. Avoid depressions where water will puddle. Remove all rocks, roots, and debris. Level the ground, excavate (see page 66), and add gravel as needed.

For a skid foundation, install a base of 6 to 8 inches of coarse gravel or crushed rock.

In dry locations you can limit the gravel to two strips under the skids, 12 inches wide by 4 inches deep. Use pressure-treated lumber for the skids, either solid timbers or three 2-bys built up so they are at least 4½ inches wide on the bottom. Angle the bottom edges of the ends. Position the skids so the outside faces will be flush with the outside edges of the shed floor. Check for parallel and square by measuring the diagonals. Stabilize the skids with rebar rods or wooden stakes along the sides. Level the skids by tamping them into the gravel at high spots, or filling in gravel underneath low spots. When you frame the floor, toenail the joists into the skids first, then reinforce the connections with L-shaped framing connectors spaced every 24 to 32 inches.

For a pier foundation, build and level batter boards for each corner of the shed and lay out string lines to represent the outside edges of the walls. Measure the diagonals to ensure that the corners are square, then mark pier locations on the ground at the four corners and at 4-foot intervals along the walls and down the center of the shed. Dig 12-inch-square footing holes at least 6 inches deep or to just below the frost line. Fill the holes with concrete and embed precast pier blocks about 1 inch deep into the fresh concrete. Using a plumb bob, align the piers with the layout lines. If possible, also level them with each other, using a long level or measuring down from the layout lines. After the concrete hard-

ens, attach 4×6 beams to the piers; use shims or 4×4 posts where necessary to level them.

An alternative to concrete pier blocks, especially where the frost line is deep, is to bury pressure-treated 6×6 posts in the ground. Excavate holes, place the posts on 6 inches of crushed rock, and backfill around the posts with crushed rock. Cut off all the posts so the tops will be level, at least 8 inches above the ground, and install girders over them, attached with steel brackets.

For a concrete slab, stake 2×8 form boards around the

perimeter. Square them by measuring the diagonals, then level them by measuring down from the string lines. Dig a trench 12 inches wide and 12 inches deep (or to just below the frost line) just inside the forms, so the slab will have a footing underneath it around the edge. Install any under-slab plumbing or wiring (including telephone wiring). Next, with gravel or sand, build up the center area to within 6 inches of the top of the forms, lay down 6-mil polyethylene sheeting over it for a moisture barrier, and

This shed has a ramp for easy access, a gable vent for air circulation, and a window for natural light.

Shed Foundations

Skid Foundation and Floor Construction

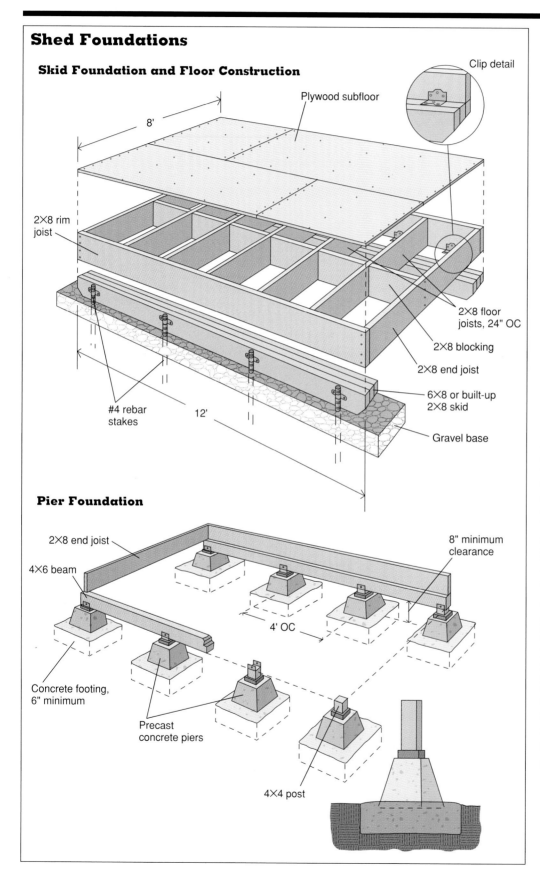

Clip detail

Plywood subfloor

8'

2×8 rim joist

2×8 floor joists, 24" OC

2×8 blocking

2×8 end joist

6×8 or built-up 2×8 skid

#4 rebar stakes

12'

Gravel base

Pier Foundation

2×8 end joist

4×6 beam

8" minimum clearance

4' OC

Concrete footing, 6" minimum

Precast concrete piers

4×4 post

cover this with 2 more inches of sand. Place two horizontal rebars along the bottom of the trench, supported 3 inches off the ground by dobies (concrete blocks), and 3 inches away from either side. Then cover the whole area inside the forms with reinforcing mesh, setting it on 2-inch dobies over the sand. After filling the trench and forms with concrete, screed it level with the tops of the forms, then smooth the surface with a wood float or darby. Place anchor bolts in the concrete around the perimeter. When the concrete has set, apply the final finish with a steel trowel or broom, depending on the texture you want. In termite areas, install a termite shield after the concrete has hardened. This is a strip of metal flashing rolled out along the perimeter of the slab (drill holes in it for the anchor bolts) and bent over the edge at a 45-degree angle. It will be held in place by the wall plates.

Floor and Wall Framing

To build a skid or pier foundation, frame the floor by installing joists over the skids or beams. Start by nailing the perimeter joists together (the two end joists and two band joists) into a box that forms the outside edge of the shed frame. Square it by measuring the diagonals, then toenail the joists into the beams with 8-penny (8d) galvanized nails.

Fill in the rest of the joists, at 16 inches on center. Toenail them to the beams with 8d nails and facenail them to the band joists with 16d nails. For a skid foundation, reinforce the joist connections to the skids with steel framing connectors. After the joists are secured, nail ⅝-inch pressure-treated plywood over them for the subfloor; use 8d galvanized nails.

Wall framing for a shed is the same as that for a home, except that shed walls and door openings are sometimes shorter to reduce the total height of the building. First, build the long walls on the floor platform and raise them into place. If the shed has a concrete slab floor, use pressure-treated 2×4s for the bottom plates of the wall, and drill holes for the anchor bolts before raising the walls. When all four walls are up, nail them together at the corners with 16d nails and nail a 2×4 cap plate over the top plates; lap the corners.

Shed Construction

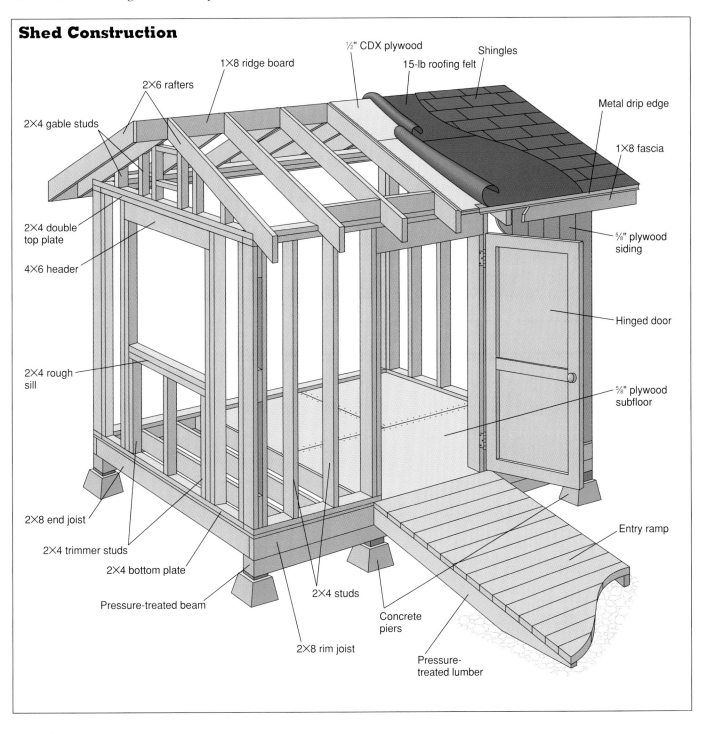

- ½" CDX plywood
- 15-lb roofing felt
- Shingles
- 1×8 ridge board
- 2×6 rafters
- Metal drip edge
- 2×4 gable studs
- 1×8 fascia
- 2×4 double top plate
- 4×6 header
- ⅝" plywood siding
- Hinged door
- 2×4 rough sill
- ⅝" plywood subfloor
- 2×8 end joist
- 2×4 trimmer studs
- 2×4 bottom plate
- Pressure-treated beam
- 2×4 studs
- 2×8 rim joist
- Concrete piers
- Entry ramp
- Pressure-treated lumber

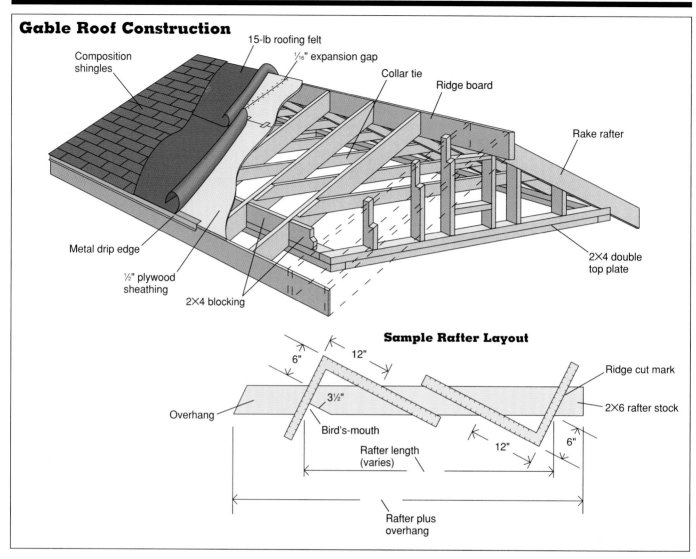

Gable Roof Construction

Composition shingles

15-lb roofing felt

¹⁄₁₆" expansion gap

Collar tie

Ridge board

Rake rafter

Metal drip edge

½" plywood sheathing

2×4 blocking

2×4 double top plate

Sample Rafter Layout

6"

12"

3½"

Overhang

Bird's-mouth

Rafter length (varies)

Ridge cut mark

2×6 rafter stock

12"

6"

Rafter plus overhang

The Roof

The most common roofs for garden sheds are gable, gambrel, and shed (a flat roof, tilted at an angle). Techniques for building a gable roof, which is the basic style in residential construction, can be applied to the other two. A 6-in-12 roof slope is adequate for most sheds, but check your plans for the appropriate roof slope. A gable roof has pairs of rafters that meet along a ridge board, and horizontal collar ties that keep the rafters from spreading apart. The rafters

are cut at an angle at the top where they abut the ridge board. This angle depends on the slope of the roof, which is measured as the number of inches of rise for every 12 inches of horizontal run (for example, 4 in 12 or 9 in 12). To mark this angle, place a framing square on the rafter stock near one end, as shown (see above), so the square intersects the rafter stock at the rise and run dimensions.

To mark the location of the bird's-mouth cut (a triangular cutout that allows the rafter to sit on the cap plate), measure

down from the ridge and mark a distance referred to as rafter length. This distance varies with the angle of slope and the width of the shed. If you don't have a carpentry manual with full rafter tables for finding this dimension, you can calculate it from the tables stamped on a rafter square. Find the row of numbers that follows "Length, Common Rafters, Per Foot of Run." These numbers are aligned under the inch marks of the square. Find the inch mark that represents the rise of your roof slope (for example, find "9" if you have a

9 in 12 roof) and note the number directly below it, which is somewhere between 12 and 22 inches. Multiply this number by the total run of the rafter, which is one-half the horizontal distance from outside the wall plate to outside the wall plate—that is, half the width of the shed—converted to inches. The rafter length is this number, less one-half the thickness of the ridge board.

After marking the rafter length on the bottom edge of the rafter, hold the square against this mark so that the two legs of the square intersect the opposite edge of the rafter at the rise and run dimensions, as shown. Using a tape measure, find the point along the square that is 3½ inches (the width of the wall plate) from the bottom rafter edge, as measured along a line that is perpendicular to the leg of the square. Mark the bird's-mouth cutting lines along this line and the rafter leg. Next, slide the square down the rafter stock and hold it where the final overhang cut will be made; the length of the overhang varies, depending on the length of rafter stock and how far you want the roof eaves to overhang the walls.

After cutting the rafter, use it as a pattern to make the second rafter. With a helper, test-fit the two rafters by holding a scrap of ridge board between them. Make adjustments, as necessary, and use the original rafter as a pattern for cutting the rest. Do not cut bird's-mouths on the two pairs of outside, or rake, rafters.

After the rafters and collar ties are in place, nail ½-inch plywood roof sheathing over them with 8d box nails, 6 inches apart at the edges and 12 inches elsewhere. Leave ¹⁄₁₆-inch expansion gaps at the ends of panels and ⅛-inch gaps along the edges.

Before you apply the roofing, nail metal drip flashing at the eaves. Next, staple 15-pound roofing felt horizontally, and add a 12- to 18-inch strip along the eaves for double coverage. Nail metal drip flashing over the felt at the edge of the rakes. Finally, apply composition shingles according to manufacturer's instructions.

Exterior Finishing

The sequence of construction varies according to what type of windows, siding, and doors you install.

Windows

Install the windows after the framing or wall sheathing is up, but before applying the siding. Staple paper flashing around the rough openings. Most windows have a nailing flange for easy installation; apply a bead of caulking to the back of the top and side flanges and set the window into place. Level it and nail the flange to the wall with ¾-inch galvanized roofing nails. Install drip flashing across the top of the window.

Siding

Staple building paper or house wrap to the outside of the framing or sheathing and install the siding over it. To install plywood siding, first cut openings for the windows and door, and notches for the rafters. Nail the panels with 8d galvanized nails, every 6 inches along the edges and every 12 inches elsewhere. Leave a ⅛-inch expansion gap between panels. Because a shed is small, you may want to use elaborate siding, such as horizontal board siding, shingles, or vertical board-and-batten siding. For an interesting effect, accent one or two small areas with fish-scale shingles or some other fancy effect.

Door and Ramp

Build a simple door from plywood or board siding reinforced by a Z frame, or buy a prehung door with a jamb set. Nail the jambs to the studs that frame the door opening. Slip tapered shims behind the side jambs to move them in or out, so the two jambs are plumb and spaced equally from top to bottom. Attach hinges to the door, set it into place, and screw or nail the hinges to the doorjamb. Install a door latch and, for security and childproofing, a lockset or a sliding bolt hasp that you can padlock.

Build a ramp outside the door. For a wooden ramp, bolt a ledger board under the door and attach two stringers to it, long enough to extend from the shed at a gentle slope. Cut the ends of the stringers at angles, so the upper end is plumb and the lower end is horizontal when each stringer is in place. Pour a concrete footing to support the lower ends of the stringers. Attach the upper ends to the ledger board with joist hangers. Cut 2×6 decking to lay across the stringers and secure it with two 16d nails at each end.

For a gravel ramp, stack a wall of railroad ties or pressure-treated timbers in front of the shed so the top of the stack is 1½ inches below the shed floor. Leave a 1½-inch gap between the shed and ties. Before setting the last timber into place, nail a pressure-treated 2×4 to the side of the shed so the top is flush with the door opening. Cover the top of the 2×4 with flashing, bend the flashing over the exposed side of the 2×4, and set the last timber up against it. Bore holes through the timbers to drive galvanized pipes down through them into the ground. Using rubble, crushed rock, sand, and gravel, build a ramp up to the top of the timbers, tamping it into place. Install an exterior door threshold in the door opening.

Trim and Finish

Trim the doors, windows, and corners with 1×4s or decorative moldings, applying caulking behind the boards before nailing them. Nail 1-by fascia boards to the ends of the rafters for a finished look, and add gutters if you wish. Paint or stain the shed, as desired. Now is the time to add a window box, shutters, trellis, weather vane, or other decorative touches.

Interior Finishing

The inside of a storage shed is not usually finished the way a house is. The exposed studs and other framing provide convenient supports for heavy-duty hangers, shelves, and racks. Spraying the interior with a flat white paint will brighten it.

Install the wiring for lights, switches, and outlets at this stage. If the walls will be covered with wallboard, use nonmetallic cable for the wiring runs. If not, up to 8 feet above the floor, enclose the wires in conduit wherever it is exposed. Place outlets 4 feet off the floor, and protect them with GFCIs.

In addition to growing vegetables and flowers, you can build or install garden enhancements. Raised beds make it easier to tend the garden. Planter boxes allow you to create gardens anywhere on your property. And other features beautify the yard or add a touch of whimsy.

Raised Beds

Raised planting beds are an attractive and easy way to level or terrace a sloping garden. Raised beds can also help you solve soil problems such as an excess of clay. A raised bed can be used in the front of your home instead of foundation plantings or to set off the front walkways or other approaches. But perhaps the best reason for a raised planting bed is that it makes it easier to tend the plants.

Raised beds are no more than large, bottomless boxes, built with railroad ties, pressure-treated lumber, redwood, cedar, or even brick or stone. You can top the planting box edge with a large plank to serve as a seat. The soil under the box should be dug thoroughly and amended with organic matter; fill the box itself with new planting soil.

There are no standard heights for a raised bed. The height depends on your design and the materials used. If using 1-by boards or 2-by planks as a frame, you need to stabilize the corners and long sides by attaching them to stakes or 4×4 posts, depending on how firm the soil is. If you build the bed by stacking

4×4s or 6×6s, the ends should overlap, log cabin style. The timbers should be toenailed in the back with 16d or 20d galvanized common nails. To hold the tiers of timber together, drill a ⅞-inch hole through at least two tiers and drive a ½-inch pipe through.

If you make a raised planting bed abutting a lawn, consider adding a 6-inch-wide brick or timber apron as a mowing strip.

Most raised beds are built by driving 4×4s into the ground and attaching boards to them. If you anticipate a problem with gophers or moles, install galvanized poultry netting on the bottom of the box before filling it with soil.

Building Raised Planting Beds

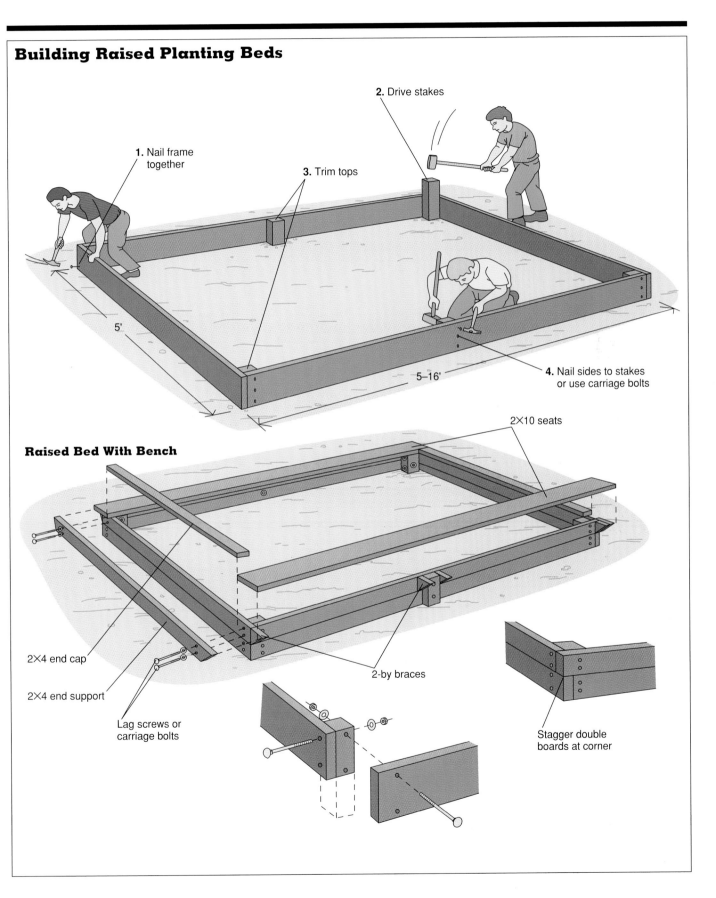

1. Nail frame together

2. Drive stakes

3. Trim tops

5'

5–16'

4. Nail sides to stakes or use carriage bolts

Raised Bed With Bench

2×10 seats

2×4 end cap

2×4 end support

Lag screws or carriage bolts

2-by braces

Stagger double boards at corner

Simple Planter Boxes

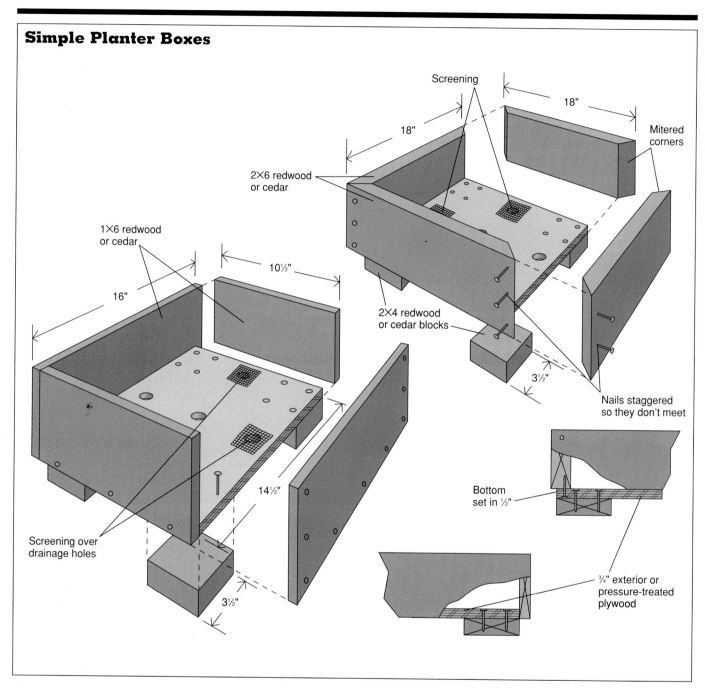

Screening

18"

Mitered corners

18"

2×6 redwood or cedar

1×6 redwood or cedar

10½"

16"

2×4 redwood or cedar blocks

3½"

Nails staggered so they don't meet

14½"

Bottom set in ½"

Screening over drainage holes

3½"

¾" exterior or pressure-treated plywood

Planter Boxes

Planter boxes are smaller and more decorative than raised beds and are used on and around decks, patios, porches, driveways, and other areas not usually associated with gardening. Some planters are permanent brick or masonry designs, others simple wood constructions. The clean, straight lines make them a natural showcase for a lush display of annuals or perennials. For these boxes you need decay-resistant wood. The best choices are redwood and cedar. Nails or screws should be galvanized.

To refine the simple wood box theme, try adding mitered corners, which will make the box look more sophisticated. If you have never done miter joints, this is a good way to gain experience with them.

To make a very large planter, construct a sturdy frame from pressure-treated lumber and sheathe the inside with ½- or ¾-inch pressure-treated plywood. For the outside, use a veneer similar to the exterior finish of your house. Be sure to drill drainage holes in the bottom of the box. To help retard decay, fit the inside of the box with a heavy-duty plastic liner.

Other Garden Features

You may want to undertake any of a number of simple garden projects to add a personal touch to the garden. Often, such additions also suggest a harmonious interplay between untamed nature and civilization. The following list should stimulate your creativity.

• Trellises for plants to climb are easy to make, using small-dimensioned lumber or even wood scraps. They are also readily available in nurseries and home centers. Simply drive the support stakes into the soil or tack the trellis to a wall or fence.

• A mailbox can be mounted on a post at a convenient place in the garden for storing hand tools, hose attachments, and other small objects.

• Many types of garden ornaments can accent your garden. Consider a birdbath, a statue or sculpture, or attractive stepping-stones.

• "Found objects" from salvage yards and other recycling sources can make interesting garden decorations. The possibilities are endless, from old tools and farm implements to architectural hardware and old street signs.

• Add natural objects such as stones, boulders, pieces of driftwood, or logs.

• Build or purchase birdhouses and bird feeders.

• Install models of buildings, boats, fairy-tale castles, or working trains.

The A-frame design of this trellis makes it easy to harvest the lemon cucumbers and beans growing on it.

A sculpture made of driftwood attached to a wooden base (top) and a concrete reflecting bowl cast in a simple form (bottom) are two examples of landscape features that are fun to make.

COMPOST BINS

As more communities and states enact laws reducing the amount of yard waste that can be dumped in landfills, compost bins become ever more popular. Their main benefit, of course, is the production of organic material to enrich garden soil.

The Basics of Composting

Walk into any garden store and you can find many styles of plastic bins, screen bins, chemicals, and thermometers to make composting as easy, or as complicated, as you wish. Books, magazine articles, and videos have been produced to explain one of the most simple of natural processes—decay.

The trick to successful composting is to keep the carbon-nitrogen ratio of the pile to about 25 to 30 parts carbon to 1 part nitrogen (when the pile has decomposed, that ratio will be more like 15 to 1, which is close to the ratio found in humus from the forest floor). Carbon is supplied by plant materials—leaves, bark, and chopped-up plants. Kitchen waste—such as coffee grounds, eggshells, fruits, vegetables, and paper napkins—also contributes carbon. To supply nitrogen, add fresh grass and manures. Avoid meats and meat products, dairy items, and high-fat foods because they decompose slowly and may draw pests.

You know the pile is cooking when you see steam as you turn the materials. If the pile doesn't produce any heat, then decomposition has been retarded. You can buy bacteriological agents to jump-start the compost pile.

Building a Compost Bin

A system suitable for most yards consists of three bins, each at least 3 feet wide, 3 to 5 feet deep, and 3 feet high. One is for raw materials, another is for processing compost, and the third is for storing finished compost. To promote aerobic action within the compost, space the boards on the sides of the bins no closer than 2 inches. If you space them more than 2 to 3 inches apart, line the inside of each bin with galvanized wire fabric to keep the compost from spilling out.

Removable front boards allow easy access to the piles as they are built up or reduced in size. Attach a 1×2 cleat to the bottom of each board, at each end, to create air spaces between boards when they are in place.

Use 3×4 posts buried in the ground to anchor the corners of the bins, or build the bins on 1×6 skids, as shown at left, so you can move the bins if desired. For lumber, use heart grades of redwood or cedar. Nail them together with galvanized nails, predrilling the ends of boards to prevent splitting.

Building a Compost Bin

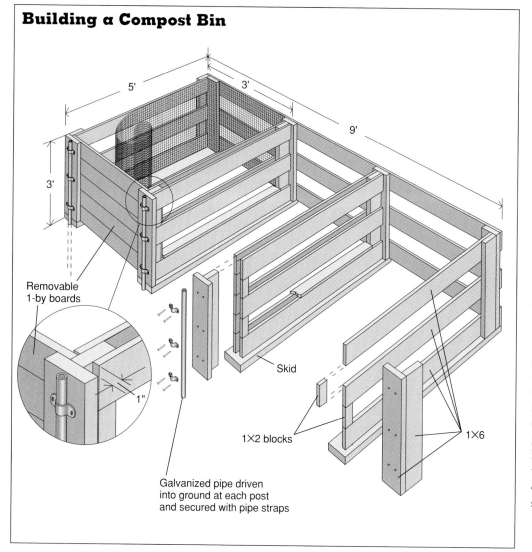

Removable 1-by boards

1"

Skid

1×2 blocks

1×6

Galvanized pipe driven into ground at each post and secured with pipe straps

PONDS AND FOUNTAINS

A garden pool can heighten the allure of any garden setting, adding shimmering highlights, serene reflections, and soothing sounds. It also provides an opportunity to grow interesting new plants.

The Joys of Water

Well-designed water features can turn an ordinary yard or garden into an attractive place to relax and enjoy nature. Whether moving or still, water always draws the eye, so it quickly becomes the focal point in the garden.

A water feature can be informal, built to resemble a natural habitat, or it can be formal, with symmetrical or geometric shapes. Build it yourself or have a landscape architect design and build it.

Size is an important element in the design of a water feature. To accent an enclosed patio, a trickle fountain in a small pool works well. In a large garden, this type of feature would be lost. Also integral to design are the plants that will grow on the surface and edges of a pond or pool.

Caution: Make sure to check local codes before building a water feature. The code may classify it in the same category as a swimming pool, in which case you must install fencing to prevent a small child from accidentally falling in and drowning.

Building a Pond

Constructing a small pond is as easy as digging a hole. It can be anywhere from 4 feet by 3 feet to 9 feet by 8 feet wide, and 1½ to 3 feet deep. Polyvinyl chloride (PVC) plastic membranes, which can be

Installing a Pond Liner

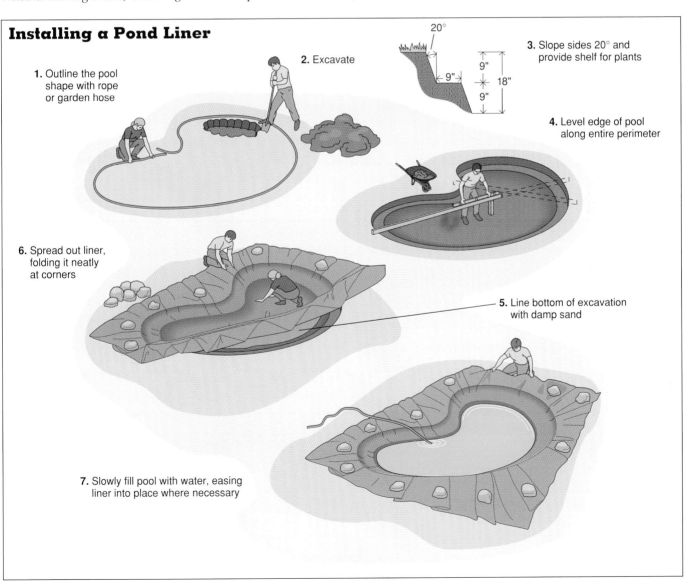

1. Outline the pool shape with rope or garden hose

2. Excavate

20°

3. Slope sides 20° and provide shelf for plants

9"   9"   18"   9"

4. Level edge of pool along entire perimeter

6. Spread out liner, folding it neatly at corners

5. Line bottom of excavation with damp sand

7. Slowly fill pool with water, easing liner into place where necessary

Finishing the Installation

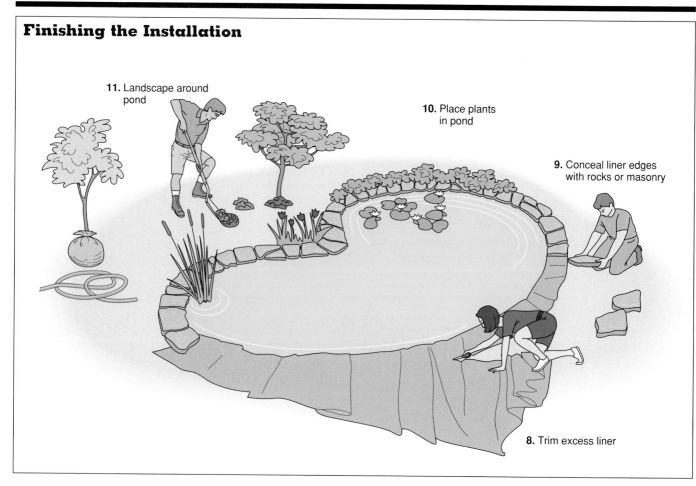

11. Landscape around pond

10. Place plants in pond

9. Conceal liner edges with rocks or masonry

8. Trim excess liner

formed to any shape, are the easiest pond liners to install. Alternatives are pre-formed fiberglass or plastic pools. When buying a liner, remember that smaller-sized pools are prone to algae.

Because water always levels itself, you need not worry about making a pool uniformly flat. However, do make sure that the rim is level all the way around. The pool edge should extend about 2 inches above grade to prevent runoff from contaminating the water.

Both formal and informal ponds are best edged with rocks or paving to keep the liner in place and to camouflage the edges. When choosing the materials for the edging—called coping—keep in mind the style of your pool. Edges for informal pools can be large rocks, smooth fieldstone, or gravel. Formal pool edges should be constructed of paving material such as brick, paving stone, or tile.

Installing a Pump

To serve as a circulating system, install a pool skimmer and submersible pump inside a plastic garbage can. Using the skimmer faceplate as a guide, cut a square hole in the can for the skimmer opening. Next to the installed pond liner, dig a hole for the can—it should be deep enough that the water level of the pond is about two-thirds of the way up the hole. Adjust the pool liner so it laps against the hole in the can, and bolt the skimmer faceplate to the can with the pool liner sandwiched between the faceplate gasket and the can. Cut out the liner inside the skimmer opening. Install a GFCI-protected outlet near the can and install a submersible pump in the can. Run a return water line from the pump outlet to the other end of the pond, where it can discharge from a rock outcropping to create a waterfall. Place a removable cover over the can.

Establishing Pond Life

When the pond is new, you may be concerned about its unnatural appearance. You can see all the plumbing, and the liner looks—well, like liner. Soon you become even more unnerved as the pool water begins to resemble pea soup. Not to worry. Cloudy water is to be expected in a newly created pool. Once the aquatic plants and fish (which you have to choose and stock) become established, the single-cell algae causing the pea soup will die and desirable filamentous algae will camouflage the pool's liner. After a few weeks the new pool will begin to flourish and look more natural. To keep the algae in check, strive for a balance of surface plants, submerged plants, edging plants, and fish.

INDEX

U.S./Metric Measure Conversion Chart

		Formulas for Exact Measures			Rounded Measures for Quick Reference		
	Symbol	When you know:	Multiply by:	To find:			
Mass	oz	ounces	28.35	grams	1 oz		= 30 g
(weight)	lb	pounds	0.45	kilograms	4 oz		= 115 g
	g	grams	0.035	ounces	8 oz		= 225 g
	kg	kilograms	2.2	pounds	16 oz	= 1 lb	= 450 g
					32 oz	= 2 lb	= 900 g
					36 oz	= 2¼ lb	= 1000 g (1 kg)
Volume	pt	pints	0.47	liters	1 c	= 8 oz	= 250 ml
	qt	quarts	0.95	liters	2 c (1 pt)	= 16 oz	= 500 ml
	gal	gallons	3.785	liters	4 c (1 qt)	= 32 oz	= 1 liter
	ml	milliliters	0.034	fluid ounces	4 qt (1 gal)	= 128 oz	= 3¾ liter
Length	in.	inches	2.54	centimeters	⅜ in.	= 1.0 cm	
	ft	feet	30.48	centimeters	1 in.	= 2.5 cm	
	yd	yards	0.9144	meters	2 in.	= 5.0 cm	
	mi	miles	1.609	kilometers	2½ in.	= 6.5 cm	
	km	kilometers	0.621	miles	12 in. (1 ft)	= 30.0 cm	
	m	meters	1.094	yards	1 yd	= 90.0 cm	
	cm	centimeters	0.39	inches	100 ft	= 30.0 m	
					1 mi	= 1.6 km	
Temperature	°F	Fahrenheit	⁵⁄₉ (after subtracting 32)	Celsius	32° F	= 0° C	
					68° F	= 20° C	
	°C	Celsius	⁹⁄₅ (then add 32)	Fahrenheit	212° F	= 100° C	
Area	in.²	square inches	6.452	square centimeters	1 in.²	= 6.5 cm²	
	ft²	square feet	929.0	square centimeters	1 ft²	= 930 cm²	
	yd²	square yards	8361.0	square centimeters	1 yd²	= 8360 cm²	
	a.	acres	0.4047	hectares	1 a.	= 4050 m²	